PITTODRIE'S SILENT ASSASSIN

Davy Johnston

ABERDEEN, NAIRN AND CALEY SHARPSHOOTER

D1609913

DESERT ISLAND HISTORIES OF ABERDEEN FC   ISBN

Aberdeen: European Era 1966-96 -A Complete Record   978-1-905328-32-1
Aberdeen: A Centenary History 1903-2003   978-1-874287-57-5
Aberdeen: Champions of Scotland 1954-55   978-1-874287-65-0

Author Donald Wilson was born in Nairn in 1955. Married with three sons, and a lifelong Nairn County supporter, he started his career as a cub reporter with his local paper, the *Nairnshire Telegraph* in 1971. In 1997 he worked for a short spell in Australia before returning to Scotland as chief reporter for the *Press & Journal* based in Inverness, and was bureau chief for the Moray edition of the *P&J* before joining Scottish Provincial Press in Inverness, where he has worked for both the *Inverness Courier* and *Highland News*. His work has been recognised with commendations at the Highlands and Islands Media Awards and he has also been shortlisted in the Scottish Media Awards.

PITTODRIE'S SILENT ASSASSIN

Davy Johnston

ABERDEEN, NAIRN AND CALEY SHARPSHOOTER

Series editor: Clive Leatherdale

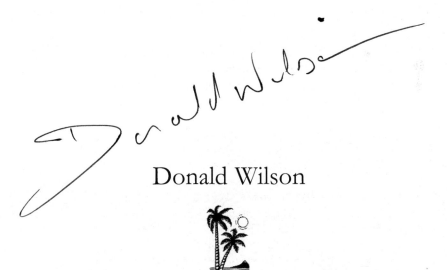

Donald Wilson

DESERT ISLAND BOOKS

First published in 2010
by
DESERT ISLAND BOOKS LIMITED
7 Clarence Road, Southend on Sea, Essex SS1 1AN
United Kingdom
www.desertislandbooks.com

British Library Cataloguing-in-Publication Data
A catalogue record for this book is available from the British Library

ISBN 978-1-905328-86-4

Printed in Great Britain by
4edge Ltd, Hockley. www.4edge.co.uk

The author and publisher gratefully acknowledge the following for the use of
photographs, some from personal collections, in this book:
Page 77: Margaret Johnston and family and W Macdonald.
Page 78: Margaret Johnston and family, Alan Stewart and James Doull.
Page 79: Alan Stewart and James Doull.
Page 80: Alan Stewart and James Doull and *Aberdeen Journals*.
Page 81: *Aberdeen Journals*.
Page 82: Margaret Johnston and family and *Aberdeen Journals*.
Page 83: *Aberdeen Journals*.
Page 84: *Aberdeen Journals* and Ian Davidson.
Page 85: Ian Davidson.
Page 86: Ian Davidson and *Aberdeen Journals*.
Page 87: Ian MacRae.
Page 88: Margaret Johnston and family and Donald Matheson,
Nairn County's official photographer.
The author would like also to express his gratitude to Nairn County's main
sponsor, Narden Ltd, for generously funding
the photographs from *Aberdeen Journals*

Contents

Acknowledgments

I have many people to thank for helping bring this book to fruition, not least my wife Fiona and my three boys, Ryan, Sean and Ross for their patience and support as I worked late into the night and at weekends over several months, neglecting family responsibilities to carry out the necessary research to compile this biography.

To Davy's widow, Margaret, and family for giving me their blessing to write this tribute and in particular his youngest son Trevor for the treasured scrapbook he handed over to me to begin my quest.

I know I would not have started writing Davy's story without being 'bullied' into it by a colleague in my office at Scottish Provincial Press's Headquarters in Inverness, Leah Williamson. Like myself, Leah is a fellow Aberdeen fan and she is a season-ticket holder at Pittodrie.

At every turn the former players, coaches and managers who worked with Davy and of course the fans I spoke to gave me nothing but encouragement. It was a privilege for me to speak to people who were my boyhood heroes and I thank them all for the gracious and positive way they responded to my appeals for information.

I also owe a great debt of gratitude to Kevin Stirling, Chris Gavin and David Innes of the Aberdeen Football Club Heritage Trust, and Duncan Davidson of Aberdeen FC Former Players Association for putting me in touch with so many of the players and people associated with the club, and to the fans and officials of Nairn County and Inverness Caley for their memories, some recorded in the chapters of this book. A special word of thanks, too, to Ian Davidson and the Bob Weir for their research. Juppy's tally certainly came as a shock to me at such a late stage of my work. Ian was an incredible font of knowledge on the Caley years and opened so many doors to me. To Hearts historian David Speed for his help in covering Davy's spell at Hearts and the staff at Aberdeen Central Library and Nairn Library where I spent many hours poring over copies of the *Press & Journal* and *Nairnshire Telegraph*.

I also want to share with readers an experience during my research at Aberdeen Central Library. It was there that I met Derek Giles, a fellow Aberdeen fan and keen historian of the club. Towards the end of my research I was trying to get a hold of Clive Leatherdale's superb 1986 book, *The Aberdeen Football Companion*. While the library had a copy available, it was their only one and they could not loan it out to me. Derek left that morning and returned half an hour later with a copy of the book. He presented it to me and said he had seen it in a nearby charity shop and, not wanting to raise my hopes, went to see if it was still there. It reminded of a similar experience when I worked at the *Nairnshire Telegraph*. An author, David Thompson, was doing research for his book *Nairn in Darkness and in Light* in the 1980s. David was desperately seeking a copy of the book *The Flowers and Fauna of a Highland Parish*. At the back of my mind I was sure I had seen a cache of these books lying gathering dust around our office and went into the attic where I retrieved several copies. David was nearly blind, hence the title of his book. But when I presented him with the copy his eyes lit up. I had the same feeling of exhilaration when Derek presented me with *The Aberdeen Football Companion* which was to prove an invaluable resource. How does the saying go? – what goes around comes around.

Thanks to my minister at Nairn United Reformed Church, the Rev Steven Manders – a dedicated Hibee – but he has my forgiveness for his encouragement and undertaking the task of proof-reading. For the photographs I thank Davy's family for access to their personal collection, my former colleague at the *Nairnshire Telegraph* Ian MacRae, Ian Davidson, *The Press & Journal*, and Jimmy Doull and Alan Stewart, who as young lads risked life and limb recording cine-camera footage and taking stills from the tin roof of Nairn County's enclosure. Finally, a special thank you to Peter and Michael Mackintosh, directors of Nairn County's main sponsors Narden, who have generously sponsored the photographs of Davy's Aberdeen years from *Aberdeen Journals* for reproduction in this book. To anyone I have forgotten, my apologies. I know your help was freely given and I want you to know it was deeply appreciated.

I also want to express my thanks to my publisher Clive Leatherdale for his wise counsel, advice and help, particularly covering Davy's spell at Aberdeen. I know without his support this book would not have offered as fulsome and accurate a reflection of Davy's career.

Thank you one and all.

DONALD WILSON
August 2010

Dedication

I would like to dedicate this book to my wife Fiona, my boys Ryan, Sean and Ross, for their love and support during my research writing Davy's story. I am so proud of them all.

Prologue

He was the most talked about Highland League player of the 1960s and early 1970s. But Davy Johnston was a footballing enigma. He was blessed with skills today's top managers would pay a king's ransom for – an eye for goal, two great feet, strength in the air and great vision.

But he turned his back on a career at the highest level in the Scottish game not once but twice. He was released by Hearts at the age of just seventeen because he was homesick. Then he caused a sporting sensation when he walked out on Aberdeen at the age of 26 after nearly three seasons at Pittodrie. Highland League football fans who saw Davy play for Nairn County in his early years and Inverness Caley after he quit the Dons will tell you without exception he was a class apart. His nutmegs, volleys and goals bewitched opponents, and memories of his artistry on the pitch are marvelled at to this day by his army of fans diminishing only by the passage of time.

One of Scotland's finest football coaches, Eddie Turnbull, told me Davy could have become as great a player as Bobby Charlton and was destined for international honours. But Turnbull was disappointed when the player whom he wanted to build his Aberdeen side around walked out of Pittodrie in 1969, never to return. It is clear many were of the view Davy had the potential to reach international stardom during a golden era for the national side.

Davy cited his health as the main reason for quitting Aberdeen. Some of his team-mates, his widow Margaret, and Eddie Turnbull have offered their views on a subject which has baffled his most ardent fans even to this day, years after his untimely passing at the age of just 61 in 2004. I will leave readers to draw their own conclusions.

I got to know Davy as a friend during our years together with Nairn St Ninian Football Club. He was my boyhood hero and when he joined the Dons I became an Aberdeen fan. Through my work as a journalist I got to know many of Davy's contemporaries, including the late 'King' Willie Grant of Elgin City and the late Rodwill Clyne who played alongside Davy in his Nairn County days. Both were great Highland League players in their own right and went on to become football correspondents for the *Sunday Post* – a must read for any follower of the Highland League football scene in years gone by. They both penned their own memoirs and paid fitting tributes to Davy – from different perspectives – Grant as an adversary, Clyne as a team-mate. For years, even before I learned sadly that Davy was terminally ill with cancer, I thought his was a story worth telling. He was a complex but modest individual – too modest I suspect to think he was even worthy of being the subject of this book. His family gave me their blessing and I know from speaking to ex-players and fans who, like me, had the pleasure of witnessing his sublime skills, his is a career indeed worthy of recognition. After much persuasion by my own family, friends and colleagues, I have finally got round to that task. I hope Davy would have forgiven me for taking this liberty of recording his story – the story of a sporting legend who, like Charlton, was never once booked in his lifetime.

He is remembered and revered today by spectators, team-mates and opponents alike who had the good fortune to witness this master goal-grabber plying his trade in the Highland League and Scottish First Division between 1959 and 1976.

Some may question why write a book about someone who 'had it all and threw it all away' and never fulfilled his destiny to become an international footballer. But in many respects that's what makes Davy Johnston's story all the more fascinating. Unlike so many football stars of the modern day, he was an individual blessed with abundant talent, but equally consumed by modesty and humility. In this book fans, team-mates, opponents, managers and coaches alike speak of an unassuming individual who enjoyed his sport but was never seduced by the, albeit modest, trappings that it could provide in that era.

When I finally started writing this book after years of procrastinating, I did so in the belief that Davy was the holder of the record number of goals scored in any one season by a Highland League player. But like any good journalist, I found you can research yourself out of a good story. And so it proved. As I built up my list of contacts and teased information from many different sources to build up a picture of Davy's career, I was shocked to find that for decades the legend that Johnston was the league's record scorer was based on a false premise.

Seeds of doubt were sown towards the end of my research by Inverness Caley historian Ian Davidson, who said he believed the record belong to Inverness Thistle and Caley centre-forward Andy 'Juppy' Mitchell. I carried out my own thorough research on Davy's record season in 1963-64 and you will find a game-by-game breakdown authenticating every goal which shows how he reached the incredible total of 73 goals that year.

But Ian, who was a great source of help to me in my research of Davy's Caley years, in collaboration with Bob Weir, an Elgin City and Highland League historian, has disproved a legend that has existed for decades, that Johnston held the record. Ian and Bob presented me with conclusive evidence that it was indeed 'Juppy' who holds this honour with 77 goals for Thistle in 1954-55. I have included a breakdown too of 'Juppy's' scoring achievements that season to set the record straight.

Readers may be surprised to learn that the Highland League does not keep records of goalscorers. To glean such information, researchers must rely on newspaper archives. My source on Davy's tally was the *Nairnshire Telegraph*, and Ian and Bob compiled 'Juppy's' dossier from the *Inverness Courier*, *Elgin Courant* and *Northern Scot*. I suspect no one can ever say with certainty these accounts are 100 per cent correct. Often reports differed between local and visiting journalists, but taking into account the balance of probability, I believe it would be unjust to 'Juppy' not to pay him his due.

While it was a shock to find Davy's 'record' usurped at such a late stage of writing this book, I remain convinced football fans in the north and north-east of Scotland will welcome his story being recorded. Although he may not be the Highland League's greatest ever scorer, no one I have spoken has ever questioned that he was the League's greatest ever player.

A Highland Legend

The history of Nairn County Football Club will forever be associated with one of Highland football's greatest legends. Many players from this northern outpost of British football may have made their fame and fortune playing in the higher echelons of Scottish and English football. But in Davy Johnston, Nairn County produced arguably not only the finest player ever to grace the turf of Station Park, but the finest footballer ever to emerge from the Highland League. His 73 goals in season 1963-64, during which he turned 21, has stood the test of time as a club record and fell just four goals short of the all-time Highland League record of 'Juppy' Mitchell set nearly a decade before.

If anyone wishes to question the authority on which I have based my assessment of Johnston's standing in the game, I will recall a conversation I had with Eddie Turnbull as I prepared the eulogy for Davy's funeral after his untimely death at the age of 61 in 2004. Turnbull told me he was convinced that had he got Davy as a sixteen-year-old he would have become as good as Bobby Charlton. He had planned to do with Davy what Manchester United did with Charlton and take him out of the forward line to play a deeper role in midfield, from where he could orchestrate games with his incisive passing and great vision.

Turnbull's credentials as a player and coach are from the top drawer. Before transforming Aberdeen to a side which was challenging the Old Firm on every front within a year of stepping into Pittodrie's managerial hot seat in 1965, he had an illustrious playing career. He was a member of the great Hibs forward line of the 1950s which was internationally renowned and became known as the Famous Five. That line-up of Gordon Smith, Bobby Johnstone, Lawrie Reilly, Turnbull and Willie Ormond struck fear in the hearts of defences both at home and on the Continent. Most of them figured prominently in Hibs' golden era of the late 1940s and 1950s when the Easter Road side were champions in 1948, 1951 and 1952, finishing runners-up to Rangers in 1950 and 1953. Such was their reputation, Hibs were invited to play in the first ever European Cup during the 1955-56 season. They reached the semi-finals, going out to French side Reims. Turnbull went on to become one of Scotland's best ever football coaches and tacticians. Known as a hard taskmaster, he took over as manager at Aberdeen in 1965 after a very successful spell with Queens Park – the same year Jock Stein joined Celtic from Dunfermline.

It was Turnbull who lured Davy away from his beloved home-town team as he began rebuilding an Aberdeen side that had been for a decade in the soccer wilderness.

Rumour in the town of Nairn had it that Johnston was a reluctant recruit to the Turnbull revolution at windswept Pittodrie on the edge of the North Sea. Nairn County's committee came in for stick from some quarters for selling the club's prized asset and fans' favourite. But Sandy Finlayson, a Nairn County official at the time, has confirmed to me that Johnston wanted to go and there was no way the club could stand in his way.

The transaction between the two clubs yielded a record fee of £8,000 for the Highland League side. Davy's widow Margaret provides a frank account of the background behind her husband joining and leaving the Dons. She admits she wished he had stayed at Pittodrie. For their young family it would have provided a much higher standard of living than would ever have been available to him on his return to his old job at the Nairnshire Laundry and as a part-time footballer. His fans simply wanted him to reach the top in a sport at which he excelled. It had taken some persuasion to convince Davy, very much a home-town boy, it was the right thing to do to take the plunge and move to Aberdeen FC when he signed for them in November 1966.

For those of us perhaps disappointed that he never fulfilled his potential and achieved international recognition, we should comfort ourselves by the fact that Davy proved for two and half seasons he could compete with the best of them, including Jock Stein's Lisbon Lions and the great players from the other side of the Glasgow divide – Rangers. Davy and Margaret already had their two-year-old daughter Sharon and new-born son David's future to think of when he signed for the Dons. Davy knew it was probably his last chance for a stab at the big time and a degree of financial security. It is evident that in his early years he was heavily influenced by his mother, who brought him up on a war widow's pension after his father Samuel was killed in the war. Samuel was a semi-professional footballer himself with Dumbarton before being posted to Fort George during the war when he met Davy's mother.

Davy was being courted by several top English and Scottish League clubs when he was just a lad of sixteen. But a year later in an interview with *Daily Express* sportswriter Hamish Black, having turned down offers from St Johnstone and Dundee and having seen a deal with Portsmouth fall through, Davy said he wanted to make football his full-time job, but the final word would rest with his mother: 'I don't intend to move from Nairn unless she gives me her blessing,' he said.

The decision to join Aberdeen some years later, however, rested with Davy and he knew that if he didn't accept Turnbull's offer, when his 24th birthday loomed, the chance was never likely to come his way again. He made that choice and, looking back, it was wrong ever to criticise the Nairn County committee of that era. They and many others who have followed them have dedicated themselves to a labour of love keeping the Station Park club alive, and it was with the club where it all began that Davy fittingly brought the curtain down on his career when the club lifted its first and only league championship title in 1976.

A modest individual, Davy was blessed with an abundance of talent which would leave many of today's obscenely overpaid professional footballers in the shade. He played 99 competitive games for the Dons, scoring 37 goals, an excellent return when you consider many of his games were played on the wing and not at centre-forward. It's an interesting statistic when you compare it with Frank Macdougall, who was hailed as the new goalscoring messiah at Pittodrie in the 1980s. In no way I am trying to diminish the impact Macdougall made at Pittodrie. Frank scored 44 goals in 68 appearances during Alex Ferguson's reign as an out-and-out striker. 'King Joey' Harper's all-time record, of course, 199 goals in 300 games, is one of Pittodrie folklore. But there were hopes Macdougall could maintain that ratio of two goals every three games for years to come. He had been signed by Ferguson from St Mirren as a replacement for Mark McGhee in 1984, a year after that glorious night in Gothenburg. For two seasons he was unstoppable, but Frank's last goal for the Dons came in May 1986 when he was just 28. Back trouble then brought his career to a premature end.

The Early Years

I was just a toddler growing up in Queenspark (known locally as Shanghai because it was built in the late 1930s during the Chinese/Japanese wars) when an unassuming youngster began his scoring exploits in 1959 at Station Park. One of my earliest childhood memories was wandering from my home in Whitelaw Crescent, so named after Viscount Willie Whitelaw's mother Winnie, who was the Town Council's Housing Convener. I got as far as William Street, just round the corner, and it was there I saw my first train billowing great clouds of steam, loudly hissing and screeching along the nearby railway line as it snaked its way along one of the longest platforms in Britain at Nairn station. Terrified and in tears I ran back round the corner to my mother. Davy lived on the same council estate as me, at the corner of Anne Crescent and Elizabeth Street. With their spacious gardens built in traditional bullrings, with one street backing on to another, everyone one knew their neighbours. The large back gardens were often lovingly tended and provided vegetables in abundance for the kitchen table – changed days from modern estates where the aim is to maximize profits by squeezing as many houses into as small an area as possible with little thought for gardens and allotments. Born during the Second World War on Saturday, 28 November 1942, Davy was brought up by his widowed mother Chrissie (née Wallace) at 1 Anne Crescent. His two-storey semi-detached house was located at the junction of Elizabeth Street, George Street and Anne Crescent just a few yards from the intersection with the main road to Cawdor. Across the road towards the end of the war years, dozens of prefabricated bungalows sprang up as the government of the day battled to provide homes for returning soldiers and their families.

Davy's home was but a stone's throw from the stark grey boundary corrugated iron fence of Station Park snaking along from the top of the station brae to the quaint, recently rebuilt, Nairn Town & County Hospital. In fact, the first-floor bedroom window of his family home looked right across the full length of Station Park and it provided a grandstand view for relatives on match days, who often watched games from that bedroom window.

Davy's father Samuel, a miner and part-time footballer with Dumbarton, was killed in 1945, in the last months of the war. Serving with the Cameron Highlanders to drive the Japanese out of Burma, he was killed by the Irrawaddy River. Some might say had his father been there to guide, influence and support him, Davy may have reached the heights in a football career his talent richly deserved.

It is not looking through rose-tinted spectacles when I say that Queenspark was a fantastic place to grow up in. Money was certainly not plentiful and if you had a fitted carpet and not linoleum in your living room you were posh – we had the latter. It was a peaceful place and the problem of drugs which has become the blight of so many communities today had not then reared its ugly head. It was a good place – lots of hard-working families – large families with lots of kids who genuinely supported each other as parents began to build lives in an era where memories of the privations and tragedies of the Second World War must have still been vivid.

Born in 1955, I was thirteen years Davy's junior. On one side of the estate we had the Riverside football pitch (to give it its full title, the King George V playing field) and the River Nairn, a wonderful natural playground where most of the kids spent their evenings, weekends and summer holidays. On the opposite side beyond the George Street boundary, which stretched several hundred yards between the old Mill Road and the football ground, we had Millbank Primary School, the railway station, the local hospital and for me of course the hallowed ground – Station Park. What more could a football-daft youngster ask for.

Between Davy's house and mine some 300 yards distance was Tommy Logan's corner shop – a store where Davy's auntie Kathy worked until she retired. More often than not the topic of conversation would turn to football, whether your purchase was a McGowan's penny caramel or a quarter pound of spam. The shop had a chewing gum vending machine on its outside wall and if you were lucky enough to insert your penny in the slot when the arrow was pointed to 9 o'clock you would get a free packet of chewing gum.

Tommy Logan himself was an avid County fan and on a Saturday afternoon he would get a break from the long hours of labour running his corner shop and join the crowds at the match. Kathy, meanwhile, would hold the fort and one of his son's, Bill, who became a trainer of guide dogs for the blind, was the message boy. On his deliveries he would stand on his bike and catch a glimpse of the action over the fence in Cawdor Road. Cars were virtually non-existent on our estate. Winter fuel was delivered by Hughie (Hutcheson) the coalman with his horse and cart. The horse, Hercules, I believe by name, had the stubbornness of a mule and on its rounds there were customers who regularly would feed it with a crust of bread. If its treat was not forthcoming, Hercules would dig its hooves in and refuse to budge until a someone provided a morsel to encourage him on his way. You could supplement your coal supply by barrowing wood down Balblair Road and back up the station brae from Gordon's sawmill. Occasionally my mother would stretch the family budget to putting a fire on in an upstairs bedroom when we moved to a bigger house in George Street. It provided a comforting glow through the night in the room I shared with my brothers as we listened to the late-night shunting of goods trains on the railway line across the road.

There were regular timely visits by James Wallace, who ran a fish and chip shop in Harbour Street. He supplemented his income with a chip van which was never short of custom as he went round the estates providing a much-valued service. There were several ice cream vendors, the Co-op grocery van, and occasionally you might be lucky enough to get a cream doughnut from Asher the baker's van, which was driven by a real gent, local football referee Andrew Melville, who was known to locals as 'Sconnie Annie'. It was an era when most mums knew how to knit a warm pullover and how to darn a pair of socks, and kids got excited when the gas man came calling to empty the meter, pouring what seemed like a treasure trove of shillings onto the kitchen table. If you were lucky enough to be in credit after the reading was checked, your mum would get a refund and some of her new found 'wealth' might be spent on buying a sweetie for the bairns.

I hero-worshipped Davy like many other lads of my generation. But I was probably too young to appreciate just how rare a talent he was in my early years. In the early 1960s youngsters had no distractions like a TV, video games and other electronic gizmos, and playing gate football under street lights was something we looked forward to in the dark winter evenings.

At weekends and in the longer days of summer, for kickabouts we sometimes ventured on to grassed areas at the corner of William Street or an area known as the town gardens opposite Davy's house in Anne Crescent – a bit of a misnomer I always thought to call it a garden. I never saw a flower grow in earnest there yet – just bare bits of earth, holes dug out for games of boolies (marbles), the odd blade of grass and a big hedge which prevented our football entering the curtilage of the neighbouring house.

One of my childhood memories growing up in Queenspark was of Davy joining in with local lads for a game of cricket at the Riverside football pitch during the summer. It's often said that many sportsmen have an eye for a ball no matter what sport they pursue. I am sure many of my contemporaries will recall Davy swinging a cricket bat and launching a full-blooded drive over the crossbar onto the football pitch, scattering the Welfare League footballers who were engaged in exchanges nearby.

Davy encouraged everyone to take part in these impromptu games at the Riverside. He had his own stumps, bails and a real leather cricket ball. One person who participated in these games was Alan Watson, who was also and remains to this day a great County fan. Alan was a stalwart of the Nairn County cricket team, which was a major force in the North of Scotland League. He recalled Davy going into the nets when he was a youngster on the town links where the cricket team still plays every summer: 'He was a natural with the bat and ball but football was always his first love and we never could persuade him to put on the whites and play in a game for Nairn,' recalled Alan.

Every Tuesday and Thursday evening myself and other young football fanatics from Queenspark would venture into Station Park to watch the players being put through their paces by Nairn's trainer and Davy's mentor Eric Geddes. Eric was an absolute gent who gave his life to Nairn County both as a player and coach and he knew what a gem he had discovered in Davy, who was already playing with his pal Chic Allan and Tommy Cowan for Clach Rangers in an Inverness juvenile league. Chic of course went on to make his mark in the Highland League and Tommy, who had some trials for English League clubs and a spell with County, went on to have a very successful career in the licensed trade. He ran the Havelock Hotel, then the Shore Inn for many years before he tragically died at a young age on the squash courts. It was Eric who put together the Nairn team of the early 1960s in which Davy flourished. One of the few coaches of that era in the Highland League with formal SFA qualifications, Eric was also the local gravedigger.

Eric lived in Queenspark near Davy, whose generation, like mine, inevitably found themselves following the fortunes of County if they had an interest in football. Bob Gordon Jnr, a retired Highlands and Islands firemaster, whose dad (also Bob) was a Nairn County committee member from the 1940s and chairman when the club won its first ever league title in 1976, was a contemporary of Davy's, and played in the Nairn reserves during that era. He fondly remembers that great Nairn side of the 1960s and how Eric built that team with Johnston, whom he had nurtured from an early age, the club's golden boy leading a formidable forward line:

'The nucleus of the side I remember came from Inverness Thistle. Tommy Sanderson, Alex Young and Jim Cameron all left Kingsmills to come to Station Park,' recalled Bob Gordon. 'Then Alex Bowman, who was transferred by Nairn in 1958 to Leicester City, returned north after three years in the First Division in England. I don't know if there was a fall-out with Thistle or if Sanderson, Young and Cameron heard things were stirring at Nairn. But their arrival at Station Park marked the beginning of an exciting chapter in the club's history.

'There was also a promising young goalkeeper, Kenny Mackenzie, who worked for the post office in Inverness and he was picked up from the Inverness Welfare League by a chap known as "Chef" MacGregor, who was scouting for Nairn in Inverness at that time. Rodwill Clyne worked for the North of Scotland Milk Marketing Board and the manager of its creamery at Nairn was Charlie Chisholm, a Nairn County committee member. Clyne was with Caley but he too joined the exodus from Inverness to Station Park. I was playing for the second team when it all started. Davy was already in the first team but he was just a lad and although it was clear he was an exceptional talent too much was expected of him. As he said himself, he wasn't Di Stefano.

'Eric was one of the few Highland League coaches of that era who held SFA badges. He was certainly a man ahead of his time, although in those days it was the committee who picked the team. Every player in those days received a postcard to tell them if they were selected, advising them to report to Station Park or be there at the appointed time for the bus if it was an away match on the Saturday. Everyone played the 'W' formation those days, with two full-backs, three half-backs and a forward line of five, including two inside-forwards. When these boys came on board, Davy really developed and the goals started to come. Rodwill was a classy player who could thread a pass through the eye of a needle and, between him and winger Alex Bowman, Davy had two players providing him with a ready supply of ammunition to score the goals. Those were halcyon days and you would have supporters buses travelling to follow Nairn every week. Club treasurers loved it when Nairn came calling because they always took with them such a large support,' continued Bob.

As a cub reporter at the local newspaper I got to know Eric Geddes. My mentor at the *Nairnshire Telegraph*, the very highly respected chief reporter Alex F Laing, faithfully kept records of every goal scored by Nairn County, something I will touch upon later. He gave me the task of visiting Eric every Saturday evening if they were away from home to get some notes on the match for publication in Monday night's *Nairnshire* edition.

It was invaluable training for me as eventually I took over from David Bain, another colleague at the *Nairnshire*, doing all the match reports at Station Park from the good times of the 1970s to the years when they struggled almost penniless but manfully in the 1980s and 90s under manager Mansell Craib.

I was always given a warm welcome by Eric and his charming wife May, who had by then moved to Sutors Avenue on a spanking new council housing estate at Boath Park. A cup of tea was always on hand and Eric would talk me through the events of the day. He always made the kids welcome at Station Park and we were delighted to act as ball-boys retrieving stray balls from the gardens of Queenspark, the hospital grounds beyond the enclosure now known as the cowshed, and the Gordon's sawmill end where hundreds of fans gathered every matchday. Often the players would be taken into the old wooden grandstand which doubled as a gymnasium to do some of their crunch curls and other stretching exercises under the watchful eye of Eric.

Built in 1937, the stand was opened by Willie Maley's great Celtic side of that era, including the legendary Jimmy McGrory, before a record crowd of over 4,048. The highlight of every training session was a bounce game at the end, and Eric would invite any of the ball-boys brave (or stupid) enough to go in goal so he could work on outfield tactics. We were just thrilled to be there on the same field as our heroes, Davy, Chic Allan, David 'Pop' Ross, another local talent unearthed by Eric, Young, Bowman and Sanderson, to name but a few.

Goalkeeper Kenny Mackenzie loved these kickabouts because he got a chance to play outfield. At 5ft 7in, Mackenzie was not tall in stature, but he had the agility of a cat, which more than compensated for his lack of height. He also had a tremendous turn of speed and, when his young protege Richard Konczak, who was keeper in the 1975-76 championship winning side began to press for a first-team place, Kenny stepped aside and played outfield in some matches – even scoring the odd goal. Aberdeen-based players like Andy Cadenhead and Billy Smith trained in the Granite City and travelled up by train on match days. The railway station, as the name of County's ground suggests, is conveniently situated on the opposite side of Balblair Road.

The training lights at Station Park were poor, but not so the playing surface, which was tended with loving care but with few resources by groundsman John Gillanders. In those days the local council thought nothing of helping out with ground maintenance. The practice games were fun for the players at the end of a gruelling training session and they provided a great opportunity for the kids to meet their heroes. The language of some of the players, it must be said, could be a bit choice, something Eric would rebuke them for, given the presence of so many impressionable youngsters.

If you were lucky enough to be picked to go in goal it could be a bit of a poisoned chalice. The players delighted in firing in shots which would send the young 'goalkeepers' scattering for safety. Few were brave, or stupid, enough to even attempt a save when shots from Johnston or Allan were raining in on goal. More than once smelling salts were called upon to bring round an unsuspecting youngster caught on the head by one of these vicious volleys – if their mums only knew. One detail I do recall about these training sessions despite my tender years was Davy's preference to train in baseball boots. He later told me he always felt he could get a greater feel from the ball through the canvas of the baseball boot, which you see many kids wearing today – but more as a fashion accessory rather than a sporting shoe.

Money was always in short supply and, rather than pay through the gate on a Saturday afternoon, most of the kids from Queenspark climbed onto the hospital wall, sneaked along the back of the cowshed and at an opportune moment, aided and abetted by paying customers already in the ground, we would hop down and mingle with the crowd. There was also a gap in the corrugated iron boundary fence at the sawmill end through which smaller kids could squeeze through. The committee, I'm sure, were well aware of this but turned a blind eye.

Sadly, after he severed his connections with the sport, to my knowledge Davy never visited another football ground, including Station Park. But I think if he were alive today he would be the first to admit that the current custodians of Nairn County are doing a good job. The old stand certainly is past its sell-by date, but the ground and playing surface is superbly maintained.

Nairn nearly went bankrupt in the early 1990s but in my role as a journalist at the *Nairnshire Telegraph* I played a small part in the campaign to save the club from going to the wall. The town rallied round and raised £70,000 in shares to clear the club's debt and start afresh. I am still a proud shareholder of the Wee County to this day. When the present chairman Peter Mackintosh took over the reins in 2000 he promised changes on and off the park.

At one time the club had aspirations of relocating to a purpose-built stadium at the Sandown farmlands, which is Common Good land. It was perhaps a pipedream and would have needed the support of the Highland Council. But inevitably that buzzword 'best value' for the taxpayers took precedence and the land is now zoned for housing, a business park and local amenity space.

I just wish sometimes, however, that government could see the bigger picture and acknowledge the important role these football clubs make to the social infrastructure of small communities. On average each year more people go to football than any other form of entertainment in the town. The club also has an active youth programme, instilling discipline and a sense of belonging to young footballers who play at different levels. In the World Cup in South Africa, politicians and senior figures in the sport and TV pundits have been beating the drum ceaselessly that there must be a lasting legacy for the young people of Africa and the game of football. I just wish that could be recognised by politicians at a local level so small clubs like Nairn County could get the help they deserve to fulfil their aspirations.

Next to Station Park lies a council depot which was once the Nairnshire Laundry where Davy Johnston laboured for years before stepping up to the Scottish League with Aberdeen. It was heavy work in a steamy environment which I have no doubt contributed to Davy's high level of fitness. Davy joined the laundry, which employed over 40 staff, straight from school. He was regarded as a reliable and hard worker at the depot, which had contracts with many of the top hotels across the north. Davy's job was to sort out their linen. The high regard he was held in as an employee could be gauged by the fact the laundry owner, Eric Brown, who was prominent in curling circles in the north, re-employed Davy immediately on his return from Hearts and Aberdeen. He later went on work as a builder's labourer and spent several years at the McDermott's oil construction site employed by Tullochs who were later to become one of the biggest construction companies in Scotland.

The laundry burned down in an overnight blaze in the early 1970s. I lived only a few hundred yards away and to my great embarrassment, as a young journalist, I never heard a word about it until I went into my office in the morning in the town centre in Leopold Street. Apparently half the street was up through the night watching the spectacular blaze while I was snuggly tucked up in my bed.

The owner, Eric Brown, rebuilt a new laundry on the site, having bought some land from the neighbouring football club – a decision subsequent committees have lived to regret. That strip of land is all that would be needed for Nairn County to build a new modern stand sufficient to meet the needs of a Highland League club. In recent seasons the Wee County has enjoyed modest success on the playing side. But just to be financially solvent is reassuring in the current economic climate and for that the present administration running the club must take considerable credit.

The future of that depot has often been the subject of discussion. If it ever does become surplus to requirements, I sincerely hope the

Highland Council lock up their lawyers and accountants in a darkened room and release a strip of land which would enable Nairn County to build a stand named after the club's greatest ever player. It would be a fitting memorial and also recognition by the council of the contribution the club plays in the life of the town.

I mentioned Mansell Craib earlier and I can't let this occasion pass without paying tribute to his services to Nairn County. He was forever working on a shoestring budget and, although they took some heavy defeats during his tenure, he was admired by everyone, including Davy, for the way he stoically stuck to his task and put a side on the park in straitened financial circumstances. As well as cobbling sides together from the local welfare and amateur ranks, he looked after the pitch with literally a shovel and a barrow, and sometimes one his old vintage tractors which were his passion. It was common knowledge that any small renumeration he received from the club was always reinvested in equipment for the players. At one stage the club was so short of funds he got workers at McDermott's oil yard to donate body warmers for players sitting on the subs bench because there was no cash available for tracksuits.

During Mansell's tenure I was invited to pick a man of the match award as I sat at the press bench reporting a league game between County and Cove Rangers. Sadly, Nairn were woeful and Mike Megginson, the Cove striker, was rampant, banging in four goals in a 10-1 annihilation.

To be fair, Billy 'Canyon' Neilson in the Nairn goal did some sterling work that night. Had it not been for him the scoreline could have been nearly doubled. But I don't think he was entirely blameless for some of the balls which went past him and landed in the Nairn net. I felt I couldn't give the award to a keeper who had just conceded double figures and so opted for the obvious choice – Megginson. That decision was greeted with disdain by the Nairn officials who couldn't see past their own keeper for the heroics he performed trying to keep the Aberdeen side's forward line at bay. I promised that night never again to choose a man of the match at Station Park and to this day never have – come to think about it, I've never been asked. Although Mansell was to eventually part company with County as it went on to a more professional footing, with a regular income stream from financial backers, the fans knew the difficulties he had faced and that he had given Nairn County his very heart and soul.

The highlight of his reign undoubtedly was the great Scottish Cup run of 1986 when he created a bit of club history by taking Nairn to the third round of the national competition – further than any manager had gone before. In the second round they met Scottish League newcomers Meadowbank Thistle, featuring an up and coming eighteen-year-old by the name of Darren Jackson, who went on to achieve stardom with Hibs, Celtic and Scotland. After a 1-1 draw at Nairn, fans piled into cars and buses for the midweek replay at the Meadowbank Stadium and Nairn triumphed 2-1 on a wet and windy night. Their prize – a home draw against First Division Dundee.

The Dundee match was played on a frozen pitch before an all-ticket crowd of 2,300. Dundee were better equipped for the conditions in terms of their footwear and coasted to a 7-0 victory. Archie Knox, their manager, was rightly furious that the match went ahead because of the dangerous condition of the pitch. He vented his spleen in the boardroom afterwards because one of his players picked up a very serious injury.

This was an issue alluded to later in his book *In a Different League* by Rodwill Clyne, who referred to another experience during his days at Nairn when the Highland League club subscribed to an SFA directive that all efforts must be made to get a pitch playable for cup-ties in the event of bad weather. Rod was harking back to his time at the club in 1963, when Nairn were engaged in another memorable Scottish Cup foray which, like the one of 1986, gave them massive exposure on national radio and TV.

On that occasion Nairn played Hamilton Accies at Douglas Park in one of the finest games ever witnessed by County fans, and who else but Davy Johnston put the County ahead after 58 minutes. Accies turned the screw as the second half wore on, but the resolute Nairn defence held out until a bad bounce of the ball went over goalie Kenny Mackenzie's shoulder twelve minutes from the end. The attendance was 5,893. There was everything still to play for, as the replay was scheduled for the following Wednesday back at Station Park. The Nairn players had gone down like nine-pins with cramp at Douglas Park, unlike the Hamilton players.

Rod believed the clamour to get the frost-bound Nairn pitch ready for the replay did them no favours. Heroic efforts were made by the Nairn committee, who put braziers on the park to thaw out the park (so history was merely repeating itself in 1986 for the Dundee game). The Nairn players hadn't recovered from the previous Saturday's exertions against the Accies, and despite valiant efforts by the home side, Hamilton squeezed home in the replay by 2-1. As a skilled and gifted player, Rod knew more than most the rigours of playing on a bog or a frost-bound surface. Better to let nature take its course he argued, and who would disagree?

In his book he pays tribute not just to Davy but to Eric Geddes: 'In Eric Geddes, Nairn had the finest trainer in the league,' wrote Rod. 'He had the vision to see the benefits of the SFA coaching courses at Largs and to my knowledge was the first to venture there.'

Rod's eyes were opened by Eric's coaching techniques. 'Gone were the long sprints, laps and physical training exercises and in came ball control, practised dead-ball situations two against two etc. Many of these innovations are still carried out to this day. The beauty of the whole system was you ran with the ball, so why not train with the ball.'

He described too how Eric chaperoned Davy when all three were on a trip to Orkney with a North Select. It was obvious even then to the powers-that-be in north football what a rare talent they had in their midst, for Davy was just sixteen. If Eric had a new move he wanted to demonstrate it was always Davy he chose to introduce it – even in the presence of vastly more experienced players.

'It's easy to now understand why he picked Davy to show how to trap a ball on the run, as he was guaranteed Davy would not let him down. Eric was the backbone of the side, even sitting on the bench,' Rod added.

Rod Clyne, who had a great Highland career himself, also gave his own assessment of Johnston, comparing him with Juppy and that other Highland League goalscoring legend, Willie Grant of Elgin. Having played with all three, Clyne said Juppy was unsurpassed on the ground and Willie in the air, but Davy had 75 per cent of Juppy's ground skills and the same of Willie's ability in the air, making him the better all-round player.

Rod also wrote a book to mark the centenary of Clachnacuddin Football Club (another Inverness club) which has battled back from a financial crisis which threatened to consign its name to the history books. I'm sure everyone in the Highlands will wish the new regime well. The Highland League without an Inverness presence would be unthinkable.

Clyne was already in the twilight of his career when he played for Nairn. He moved on to Caley after two and half seasons at Nairn as second team player-coach. He brought many of Eric's techniques with him to nurture the crop of young talent at Telford Street.

The Swinging Sixties

The music revolution of the 1960s was something most teenagers of that era got caught up in, and Davy was no exception. Retired painter and decorator Billy Gibson grew up with Davy and he was able to give an insight into their childhood days in Queenspark. Billy was with local group called 'The Magnificent 7', so named after the famous Western starring Yul

Brynner. The band later changed its name to 'The Sinners', and Billy recalls the day the band recruited his boyhood pal as a singer:

'My mother and Davy's mother pushed us in our prams together up the riverside. So we knew each other from an early age and we both went to Millbank School,' recalled Billy. 'Davy was hanging about with the band and we realised one night he had a bit of a voice so we asked him to try a couple of numbers. I remember clearly the first time hearing him sing. It was *Sea of Heartbreak* by Don Gibson (released in 1961, when Davy was eighteen), and Davy sung it round at George Macleod, our bass guitarist's house, in Elizabeth Street. He was a natural. He had a great voice and when he performed for the first time at the Beat Club, which met in the Public Hall on Sunday nights, he went down a storm. He would come round to our house on a Saturday morning when I was still in my bed and ask my mother if he could play my records.'

The Public Hall was a favourite venue for many up and coming bands of that era, including Status Quo, The Beatles, Marmalade, The Who and Herman's Hermits. It also had the less enviable reputation as the scene of many scraps between rival gangs from the neighbouring towns of Inverness and Elgin.

'Davy loved rock and roll music and knew all the hits of that era,' added Billy. 'The band performed all over the north, from Tain and Clachnaharry to Keith, Buckie, Elgin, Forres and Inverness and it was great fun.'

Billy said that, to his close friends, Davy was always outgoing and good fun to be around:

'But there was a shy side to him as well. He was a real showman and loved being on stage and of course on the football field. But he was always reserved when in company of people he didn't know or people who were in authority. He wasn't powerfully built when he was a kid but you could see he had exceptional skills at football and he always excelled at sport. He was a good student when we moved on to Nairn Academy.

'I wasn't a great football fan but there was a group of us who would hang out together – John Dick, Scotty McPherson, John Main, David Stevenson, Andy Matheson, Jimmy Chisholm, Ronnie McHattie, Jimmy Mirzan, Ali Farquhar and George Macleod. We were all neighbours and Jimmy's brother Jock was the manager of The Sinners and got the band a lot of gigs. We would jump the hospital wall on training nights at Station Park and, even though he was just a kid, Davy would go onto the park and play with the County first-team players. He would run rings round them so I suppose they had their eye on him as one for the future from a very early age.'

John Dick had a spell as a goalkeeper with Nairn and he later teamed up with Davy when he was on the committee of St Ninian. Billy Gibson recalled how, when Davy came home for a break during his teenage spell with Hearts, he often wore the club blazer with great pride:

'We would go to the putting green at the links and then off to the pub for a drink but Davy would only have a couple of stouts in those days. He never was a big drinker. When he came back to Nairn and began playing for County we continued to hang out together. I went to see some of the big games and he was fantastic. I think to some extent he enjoyed my company because I wasn't mad on football and it wasn't a subject of conversation when he was with me. Everyone else just wanted to talk to him about football and tell him what a great game he had played the previous Saturday. At times it got a bit much and when he was with me we would dive into a shop doorway because he saw someone coming who would want to stop and talk about his last game. There was a shy side to Davy. But among friends he was great company.'

George Macleod, who was bass guitarist in The Sinners, was a keen football fan and was one of the gang who went to the riverside pitch every Sunday where they would play for hours on end. He recalls in 1961 when Davy returned from Hearts for his summer holiday he told him he wasn't going to go back to Tynecastle:

'He told me he was homesick and missed Nairn. I told him he wasn't wise. Most boys would give their right arm to get the chance he was getting. A few days later I was going home when I saw this big limousine in our street, I think it was a Jaguar, sitting outside Davy's house. It turned out it was Tommy Walker, the Hearts manager, who had come up to Nairn to persuade him to return to Tynecastle. He did, but of course homesickness got the better of him and a few months later he returned to Nairn.'

One big attraction for kids from 'Shanghai' was the nearby river. Many took up angling and followed a legitimate course in this healthy pursuit, including Billy Gibson: 'I took Davy once to the Whinnieknowe pool but I think he got bored after about five minutes. He disappeared to the football pitch nearby to play with his mates,' Billy recalled.

The River Nairn is a great spate river and has a thriving angling association. Lots of families supplemented their income by catching salmon, by means both fair and foul, and selling them on to the local hotel trade which was eager to have the delicacy on their menu for summer visitors. Many summer nights were spent at the Jubilee Bridge on the lower reaches of the river, tracking the salmon coming fresh up from the sea. You could see their wake in the moonlight shining on the river through the arches of the railway viaduct. Waiting for grilse and salmon were a posse of poachers by night, and anglers by day.

My own mother would often go into a panic as she woke in the morning to find three, sometimes four, salmon lying in the bath after night-time excursions to the river by her offspring. Skulking into the trades-man's entrance of west end hotels, we would quickly strike a deal with the chef, the salmon would be handed over and the proceeds went back home to supplement the family income.

I make this revelation without fear of retribution. Poachers turned gamekeepers there are in abundance in Nairn today. But my lips are sealed as to their identities. Although salmon poaching will always be part of the Highland way of life, the practice declined sharply as the need to conserve stocks became apparent, and of course farmed salmon brought prices plummeting.

Davy makes Nairn County debut

Even before he made his debut in a Nairn County shirt, Davy was being tipped for stardom. English First Division club Portsmouth, who were headed for relegation, were the first senior club to come knocking on his door when he was playing outside-left for the Nairn County 'A' team. The local newspaper reported in January 1959 that Davy, then just sixteen, had been invited to join the groundstaff at Portsmouth and his departure to Pompey was imminent. However, that deal fell through for reasons unknown.

The following month he made his debut in the Nairn County first team at outside-left. On 28 February 1959 his name appeared on the Station Park team-sheet for the first time. The Nairn team was struggling in the lower reaches of the league. And with several injuries to contend with, the young Johnston was pitched into the side to face Lossiemouth in the second round of the North of Scotland Cup.

It was no *Roy of the Rovers* fairytale debut. County went down 0-2 and their cup hopes were shattered. But the youngster had done enough to serve notice that he was there to stay. And in the early 1960s Davy was to play his part as County went on to dominate this competition, winning the trophy three times in four years.

Battling to avoid the wooden spoon in the Highland League, Nairn were up against the might of Elgin City the following weekend. Given little chance following their cup defeat by Lossie, the return of striker Gordon Brand gave Nairn a more potent threat up front. Although he did not figure on the scoresheet, the boy Davy contributed to a well deserved 3-2 win.

Missing from the Nairn team that day was a school pal and lifelong friend of Davy, Chic Allan – or Charles to give him his proper name. A chunky player built like a battering ram, Chic was not short in the skills department either. He had already broken into the Nairn first team and the two school pals were to form a deadly striking partnership with Nairn and later at Telford Street with Inverness Caledonian (Caley).

Chic Allan was tragically killed at the age of 30 on 27 July 1972 in a freak accident, falling from a hotel window in Stornoway. As Davy's widow will recall later in this book, Chic's death had a devastating effect on her husband. They had been through school together and blossomed as the two finest players Nairn ever produced. Between Davy's spells at Nairn and Caley in the early and late 1960s and early 1970s, they formed one of the most lethal double acts ever to grace north football. Their bond of friendship was strengthened on Johnston's return from Aberdeen in 1969 to sign for Caley. Although he later trained in driving diggers on building sites, Davy never held a driving licence, so Chic acted as his 'chauffeur' to and from Telford Street. Davy eventually lost his appetite for the game and was at the centre of a further controversy when he walked out on Caley. He was later released to play for the club which was always his first love, Nairn, and it was fitting that he should be part of the club's first title-winning season in 1975-76 before ending his playing career at the age of just 33.

It was on Wednesday, 15 April 1959 against Clach at Grant Street Park, Inverness, that the first of his 286 goals was scored in Nairn colours was chalked up by Johnston. Brand had already given Nairn the lead in the 73rd minute and it was Brand who provided a telling pass eight minutes from time which saw Davy strike home an unstoppable drive from eighteen yards – the kind of goal which was to become a hallmark of his career.

Now an automatic choice in the side, ten days later Davy sparked a 5-1 rout of title challengers Keith. He had already sent one shot crashing against the bar before opening the scoring with just twelve minutes gone. The *Nairnshire Telegraph* described the goal thus: 'with considerable guile he lobbed the ball with precision past a defender into the net to put Nairn one up.'

Nairn were at the foot of the table, battling desperately to avoid finishing bottom, and the following week they went 2-0 up against eventual league champions Rothes, but the Speysiders battled back to claim the points with a 4-2 victory.

However, Johnston and his team-mates were rewarded for their spirited late run when, in their final game of the season, they secured a 3-2 win over Inverness Thistle which elevated them to second bottom with nineteen points. Johnston finished his debut season having played nine league games (scoring three goals) and one North Cup-tie.

Lots of questions were asked by fans at the annual general meeting which followed. But the erratic form of the 1958-59 season was put down to a bout of injuries. Club chairman Tom Walls also made strong denials that the club had paid a £70 signing on fee for a player that season. At the same meeting it was reported that Nairn's trainer Eric Geddes had returned from an SFA coaching course at Largs, which had opened up for him a completely new outlook on training methods.

Although it had been a traumatic year for County, the green shoots of recovery were showing and Eric Geddes went on to build a side which was to become a major force in the Highland League. Davy Johnston was also going to take centre stage after his spell at Hearts and his scoring exploits were ultimately to lead to his move to Pittodrie.

The 1959-60 season got off to a good start for Nairn, with Johnston and Allan, still just teenagers, beginning to emerge as a highly productive partnership. Johnston scored the Nairn goal in a 1-1 draw with Forres Mechanics in a Highland League Cup-tie.

The following week it was the traditional Nairn Games Night derby match. Again, Forres Mechanics provided the opposition at Station Park in the return leg of the cup competition. Nairn were runaway 5-2 victors before 1,600 fans and Johnston proved it was not just with his feet that he could find the net when he scored with a splendid header. But the erratic form which dogged them the previous season was again in evidence and they had to wait until October before a 3-0 win over Buckie gave them their first league points of the season.

In November that year there were reports that Davy had been interviewed by George Swindin's Arsenal, and Scottish clubs including Dundee and St Johnstone were monitoring his progress. The Highbury club were back again in January but no offer was made.

In March 1960 the powerful Elgin City side were still carrying the banner for north football against mighty Celtic in the third round of the Scottish Cup. The biggest shock in Scottish football was on the cards with Elgin leading 1-0 eight minutes from time before a crowd of 11,200 fans at their home ground, Borough Briggs. But the Hoops saved the day and their blushes, scoring two late goals to win 2-1.

Nairn continued to toil and finished the season second from bottom but Davy, just seventeen, had played 38 games, scoring eight league, two

League Cup and two Qualifying Cup goals and he was attracting a lot of interest from senior clubs.

The annual general meeting of Nairn County in May had fans expressing their disappointment at the team's poor form. A loss of £47 on the season was reported and chairman Tom Walls warned 'gates will need to improve if County are to continue as a senior side'. How many clubs around the country would be delighted with a balance sheet which showed their annual loss was equivalent to the price of fifteen pies and Bovril in today's money. With wages about £10 a week for the average working man, I suppose this puts things into perspective. Even with such a modest deficit, the alarms bells were ringing, demonstrating fiscal responsibility sadly lacking in the management of many clubs today.

Before the 1960-61 season got under way, Nairn's Gordon Brand and Davy were in a North Select under the wing of trainer Eric Geddes selected for a friendly in Orkney. The Highland League side triumphed with Brand (three) and Johnston among the scorers.

Hopes were high for a better start when Elgin City came calling to Station Park on Games Night. But 'King' Willie Grant ran amok, scoring all five goals in a 5-1 rout. This was to be the season Grant finished his season with 65 goals and a week later Nairn were being put through the wringer again by Elgin. A hat-trick by Willie had Elgin strolling 3-0 by half-time and they went on to rack up an 8-1 win.

Hearts make their move

For Johnston, though, the prospect of senior football was beckoning. His performances continued to impress despite the team's inconsistent form and his first chance of big-time football was just around the corner. In September 1960 those clubs stalking Johnston should have been alerted when he ruthlessly put Wick Academy to the sword with five goals in a Qualifying Cup-tie. Davy took just twenty seconds to open the scoring in a 6-2 demolition against a spirited side from the far north. A penalty goal in a 3-1 win over Ross County in the semi-final of the Inverness Cup was followed by two more goals in a 5-2 league win over Huntly.

Tommy Walker, manager of Scottish champions Hearts, was tipped off by Nairn exile John 'Barney' Morrison, who was on the Tynecastle club's books in the 1950s. It later emerged Celtic had a scout at the Huntly match, but they were either slow to move or didn't fancy the player – either way, not good judgement on their part. Hearts trainer John Harvey and Morrison were in the stand observing Johnston's two-goal

performance against the Christie Park side and the Edinburgh club prepared to make their move. Other clubs may have taken their eye off the
ball, too, as far as Johnston's progress was concerned, and Walker was the
first to close in.

On Thursday, 28 October 1960 the Hearts boss travelled north up the
A9 himself to meet the player and Tom Walls, the Nairn chairman. Walls,
a local dentist, had earlier resisted efforts by other south clubs to get
Johnston to go there on trial. He was firmly of the view that any player's
ability could be judged adequately by his performance at Highland
League level. Such trials, said Walls, did nothing but cause unrest for both
player and the club, especially if no deal materialised.

The talks between Walls and Walker clearly were amicable. The negotiations took just twenty minutes and a fee of £600 was agreed between
the clubs and Johnston's personal terms were settled. Walker returned
south immediately, delighted at having secured a player he hoped would
restore the glory days at Gorgie Road as the golden era of Alfie Conn and
Jimmy Wardhaugh came to an end. The following day Johnston registered as a Hearts player and Davy's employer at the Nairnshire Laundry,
Eric Brown, allowed him to quit work immediately to pursue his dream.

Johnston's tally of nine goals in twelve Nairn games at the start of the
1960-61 season brought his Nairn total to 27 goals in 51 first-team
games. He left for Tynecastle, a month short of his eighteenth birthday,
with the best wishes of the club and the whole population of Nairn, who
dearly hoped he would make a success of his career in the highest echelons of Scottish football.

Davy shared digs with a young up-and-coming goalkeeper who went
on to make over 500 appearances for the Jam Tarts, and was to win international honours for Scotland. Jim Cruickshank from Glasgow had
signed for the Edinburgh club around the same time as Davy and went
on to become a hero with the Gorgie Road faithful. But homesickness
was to take its toll, and within a year Davy would be back beginning
another journey with Nairn County.

After three successive wins, before Johnston's departure, County's
first game without their talisman was always going to be a severe exami-
nation. They lost 0-2 to Clach at Grant Street and the *Nairnshire Telegraph*
reported: 'the Nairn forward line was less menacing with the absence of
Johnston.'

With the transfer cash, however, the squad was strengthened with a
few new signings. Nairn's season blew hot and cold, but before the curtain came down they reached the final of the North of Scotland Cup
against Elgin. The first encounter ended in a 2-2 stalemate but that man

Willie Grant was on song again with a hat-trick as Elgin triumphed 3-1 in the replay at Mosset Park.

Nairn, however, after three seasons struggling in the league basement, finished in a more respectable ninth place with eleven wins, five draws and twelve defeats in a league of fifteen teams.

A Year at Tynecastle

It is clear from all accounts that Johnston's spell at Tynecastle was an unhappy one. He had arrived at a club in transition as the great era of Conn, Wardhaugh and Bauld was coming to an end. Sandy Finlayson recalled: 'Davy went to with Hearts when he was just seventeen. Clubs didn't look after young players as well as they do nowadays. Davy had a lot of spare time on his hands to brood. While the other players had their families and friends, Davy was a young lad from a small town in a big city. He would train in the morning and had the afternoons and evenings off. Some young lads may have been able to handle it but Davy couldn't. It's as simple as that. When we heard he was coming back to Nairn we were sorry in one way but delighted in another because we knew with a year of full-time training behind him he would have matured as a player and would be stronger than ever. Tommy Walker, I have to say, was a perfect gentlemen and very understanding about the whole situation. He didn't want to lose Davy because he knew his potential. Having an unhappy youngster was no use to him and he helped facilitate his move back to Nairn. But obviously built into the agreement was the proviso that he would not be allowed to sign for another Scottish League side.'

The day after he signed for Hearts, Johnston was pitched into the reserve side against Motherwell. A Nairn man living in Edinburgh, Ross Johnston (no relation), went along to see him perform. Speaking later to the *Nairnshire Telegraph*, Ross described Davy's first game in Hearts colours: 'Johnston gave Hearts fans a grand show and they were all delighted to think that at long last they had a first class left-winger. I waited after the game to say "hello" to him and wish him good luck – I am indeed looking forward to seeing him in action again soon.'

Nairn's chairman received a phone call on the Saturday night after Johnston's first game for the reserves to be told he had made a favourable impression, laying on three goals.

Davy's first-team debut on the evening of Monday, 7 November 1960 was against a British Army side. He scored two of his side's three goals in a 3-2 win, including the clinching goal. Walker no doubt was suitably impressed, for Johnston figured in the starting line-up on 12 November for an away fixture against Kilmarnock – his Scottish League debut.

Although he was not on the scoresheet, Hearts won the match 2-1. A former school-mate of Davy's caught up with him at Rugby Park and got a lift home to Glasgow on the Hearts team bus. Local farmer Bob Pottie, whose family farmed at Easter Dalziel, Dalcross, was at agricultural college in Glasgow during Davy's spell with the Tynecastle club. They had played together in a Moray, Nairn and Inverness Schools Select which had crushed Banffshire Schools 10-0 at Elgin when they were fifteen:

'He was head and shoulders above everyone at schoolboy level,' Bob Pottie recalls: 'I remember one school team I played in got a 10-0 thrashing at the Cromal Park in Ardersier. We had to play a return match and we were determined not to go through the same humiliation, so we pulled Davy into the side. I think we broke the rules because he had already left school. They certainly didn't steamroll us in the second game. They won again but I remember it was a very close match.'

Further evidence of Johnston's early promise could be found in the Nairn Academy school magazine of 1957, which showed he played for both junior and senior XIs. And in a Scottish Schools Cup-tie at Brechin's Glebe Park, Davy scored six goals for Moray and Nairn in a 9-4 win over Kincardine and North Angus. Bob Pottie and another Nairn Academy pupil, Ian Cruickshank, were in the team that day. All three lads played in the next round, when they went out after a hard-fought match, 1-4 to Dundee Schools.

Bob Pottie went on to become a keen amateur athlete and well known in Highland curling circles. He still has fond memories of the day he saw Davy make his league debut for Hearts at Rugby Park. Having travelled by bus from Glasgow down to Ayrshire he hoped he would get the chance to speak to Davy because there had already been rumblings that his old school team-mate was unsettled:

'My father Peter was on the committee at Station Park and he had heard that Davy was homesick so he thought it would be good if we could catch up with each other and have a chat. After the game I approached some of the Kilmarnock officials and told them I was a friend of Davy's and they let me in to speak to him. The next thing I knew Davy arranged for me to travel back with him on the Hearts team bus as far as Glasgow. My dad was a great admirer of Davy and his best mate Chic Allan. They were a fantastic partnership and worked together hand in glove. Often Chic would act as the decoy and make the space which would allow Davy space to score another goal. I saw them play together at Nairn and Caley and they were tremendous.'

'Something I recall they did at Telford Street I had never seen done before and never seen done since. Caley had won a penalty and Chic stepped up to take it. But instead of shooting for goal he passed it to the side and Davy, who was in on the ploy, nipped into the box and stuck it past the keeper who was completely wrong-footed. I don't even know if it was legal but that definitely happened.'

This tale was verified by Ian Davidson who was at the game and had never seen anything like it before.

Davy went on to play a total of seven games, scoring three goals, for Hearts and he was never on a losing side. His first Scottish League goal was scored in a 1-1 draw at Starks Park against Raith Rovers on 1 April 1961.

Little was said about his departure from the Scottish champions, other than the young Johnston was homesick. But in a later interview after he walked out on the Dons, Davy reflected on these days at Tynecastle. He told *Evening Express* features writer Innes Stephen that Hearts were in trouble that year (they finished seventh) after several very successful seasons: 'A lot of the established players didn't exactly go out of their way to help me. I suppose they were more worried about keeping their own places. With me being just a raw youngster from the Highlands, I never really settled down and I asked to be released and went back home to Nairn. I was quite content with my job at the laundry.'

Of Davy's seven matches for the Hearts team, his debut, that friendly against a British Army side, had its highlights screened on television. If only video existed to show the young Davy in action, but of course it did not. Johnston's full record with Hearts reads:

7 November 1960 v British Army, home (3-2 win) Davy scored two goals;
12 November 1960 v Kilmarnock away (2-1 win);
19 November 1960 v Clyde away (1-1);
26 November 1960 v Raith Rovers at home (1-0 win);
1 April 1961 v Raith away (1-1) Davy scores first Scottish League goal;
8 April 1961 v Third Lanark home (1-0 win);
20 April 1961 friendly v Chirnside United away (3-0 win).

Station Park homecoming

Back at Station Park, Nairn had a disastrous start to the 1961-62 season. But by the end of that campaign a clutch of new signings and the return of the exiled forward saw the green shoots of recovery begin to emerge for a new-look County side which was to become a major force in the Highland League.

The season began in wretched fashion with a bruising 0-5 defeat by Clach on 12 August. Even the big Games Night crowd at Station Park a week later didn't lift the spirits of the gloom merchants as Forres Mechanics cantered to a 4-1 victory. Ross County, Keith, Fraserburgh, Rothes and Huntly and Lossie all recorded wins at Nairn's expense and a crushing 1-10 defeat at Buckie sparked calls for an all-local side by fans who feared things couldn't get any worse.

Five newcomers were to appear in the Nairn line-up the following week when they faced Buckie. The only consolation was that the margin of the defeat was not quite so embarrassing – 1-5. That was followed by a 2-3 home defeat against Lossie and then out of the blue came the news that Johnston was returning to the fold from his year's exile at Tynecastle. Still without a point, Nairn travelled to Lossie on 14 October 1961 and Johnston was on the team-sheet. Fans had learned the day before the match that Hearts had agreed to release Davy for family reasons.

There was speculation that Nairn had repaid Hearts between £200 and £300 to get Johnston back – a lot of money when you consider the fuss over a £47 deficit a couple of years before. Safeguards were certainly put in place by Hearts so he could never sign for another Scottish League side (a clause later rescinded by Hearts when approached in 1966 by Eddie Turnbull) – but the Nairn faithful were just thankful to have a player who could potentially bring happy days to Station Park.

It was no fairytale debut at Lossie as the Coasters edged home 2-1. But the following Saturday, 21 October 1961, a Johnston header cancelled out an early strike by Peterhead, and Nairn's never-say-die skipper Fred Milne snatched the winner in the 88th minute.

In his first four games after his return, Johnston (not yet nineteen) scored seven goals and Nairn picked up another two points with a 5-1 win over Huntly. Four of those goals came against the Christie Park side. While Johnston took the plaudits for his scoring prowess, match reports acknowledged that is was not just his eye for goal which made him such a rare talent. His positional sense and precision passes to team-mates inspired the side and it was this element to his game that Turnbull recognised when he was at Aberdeen as one of Davy's greatest gifts. Even this early in his career, Johnston and Chic Allan were beginning to forge a good understanding that was to stand them in good stead in the years to come.

The following week (18 November), however, a crushing blow was in store for Johnston and Nairn. Davy suffered a broken ankle in a 2-2 draw with Inverness Thistle, an injury that was to keep him out of the game for nearly three months. Nevertheless the team battled on and proved with victories over Clach, Caley, Rothes, and Inverness Thistle that they were going to be no pushovers, even without their ace marksman.

Johnston made his return on 10 February 1962 against Elgin but I suspect he wished he didn't. City ran riot with Willie Grant scoring four times in a crushing 9-0 victory for the men from Moray.

Nairn played out the season with a mixed bag of results. But Johnston was beginning to find the net with consummate regularity, one of the highlights being a hat-trick in a 7-0 rout of Inverness Thistle.

With fifteen points to show for their efforts and a second from bottom finish, it was a disappointing end to the season – but in the seventeen games he played since his return from Hearts, Johnston had bagged seventeen goals, one fewer than the club's leading scorer for the season Jackie Shields, who had eighteen.

Bill Mitchell, the club treasurer, reported at the AGM that the season was a heartbreak for everyone concerned. One suggestion put forward by committee member Jim Wilson was that the club should invest in a personality player from the south to pull in the crowds – the reality was they had one sitting under their noses. And in the next two seasons he was going to score 120 goals and play a major part in one of the most successful periods in Nairn County's history.

Mitchell assured everyone at the meeting that there were no signs of despondency, and the signing activity of that summer bore this out as Nairn finally put together a team that could compete on all fronts. Winger Alex Bowman, who had been sold to Leicester City by Nairn in 1958 for a £500 fee, had returned north. Although he turned out for Inverness Thistle, he pledged his future to Nairn. Tommy Sanderson (half-back) and Alex Young (full-back) moved to Nairn from Inverness Thistle during the close season and they were followed by another Kingsmills favourite, silky midfielder Jim Cameron. The exodus of players from Inverness continued when veteran Rodwill Clyne (striker) moved from Caley to Station Park. It wasn't long before Eric Geddes, with this wealth of talent at his disposal, transformed the team into trophy winners.

1962-63 started off with a 1-4 Morganti Highland League Cup defeat at Forres, but the new-look Nairn side began to gel and a 4-1 win against Lossie, followed by a 2-0 win against Forres in the return leg of the cup, raised the aspirations of the long-suffering fans. Two tough games against Elgin were next on the cards, with a narrow defeat and a draw keeping them in contention for the next stages of the competition. That was secured with a 4-3 win in midweek at Lossie, which also earned Nairn an even bigger carrot – a place in the Scottish Cup. And that was a journey which was to become part of the club's folklore.

Nairn obliterated Clach 8-3 in September in the league, with Johnston the star of the show with five goals, bringing his tally for the first nine games of the season to fifteen. There is no doubt his time at Hearts was not a happy one, but the benefits of full-time training were going to pay big dividends for Nairn in the years ahead.

Rod Clyne, the former Caley skipper, made a promising debut for Nairn that day as the Station Park club continued to strengthen its player pool for the club's first serious challenge for honours in years. Clyne scored an equalising goal in the semi-final of the Qualifying Cup against his old club at Telford Street, and in the replay at Station Park Nairn were coasting 2-0 when the Inverness side hit back to level the game and take it to a second replay.

There was a bizarre sequel to this match as Nairn fans laid the blame on an over zealous bobby for costing them their place in the final. A section of the Nairn fans had been making their presence felt by blowing a horn to spur on their side. But the PC on duty told them to desist or they would be charged with a breach of the peace. In letters to the *Nairnshire Telegraph* angry fans noted both Caley goals were scored when the horns were silent – so there you are. It was nothing to do with the fact, perhaps, that Nairn took their foot off the gas. There was no hiding the anger of the County fans, however, who said the previous week at Telford Street, they faced no such constraints as they noisily got behind their team. Caley went through with a 3-1 win in the second replay at the neutral Clach ground but lost the final to 1-3 to Keith.

Johnston's scoring feats, however, were again attracting attention and First Division Sheffield Wednesday formally approached Nairn president Walls after the first replay at Nairn. Walls politely told the visitors that the player wasn't for sale and that Davy did not want to leave Nairn.

In November a new goalkeeper appeared on the Nairn team-sheet. Kenny Mackenzie, who was signed from the Inverness Welfare League, made his debut in a 3-2 win over Fraserburgh, courtesy of a hat-trick by Johnston. Mackenzie became a hero with the Nairn fans before handing over the mantle to a young rising star, Richard Konczak. I've no doubt it gave Mackenzie great pleasure when his young protégé was to play a heroic part in Nairn's first and only championship success of 1975-76. Mackenzie finished his career with Chic Allan and Johnston at Caley.

In their next game County were up against the mighty Elgin and again the unstoppable Willie Grant took centre stage with a hat-trick in his side's 4-3 victory. Johnston, Shields and Clyne were the Nairn goalscorers, but even in defeat the home fans knew they were on the threshold of a great new era. A 3-2 win over Deveronvale was followed by a 5-2 victory over Inverness Thistle, the inspirational Johnston scoring a hat-trick. This gave Nairn a healthy return, after the previous season's poor showing, of ten points from their first eight games.

Into December, and Nairn proved they could compete with the best when they beat Elgin 2-1 at Station Park and followed that up with another narrow 1-0 home win over Ross County. With the Scottish Cup draw beckoning and the team in such strong fettle, spirits and aspirations were high. Nairn received a bye into the second round, where they were paired with high-flying Second Division Hamilton Accies. The Academicals made it to the third round after a replay at Nairn, but more about that unforgettable chapter in the club's history later.

County finished the 1962 calendar year on a high with a 5-2 win over Forres after being 0-2 down and were proclaimed as the best Nairn side since the one that challenged for the title in 1938-39. The Nairn revival against Forres was inspired by the 'pulverising right wing sallies of Johnston', according to the match commentary. His season's tally was already standing at 29, and as well as the new signings of Clyne, Bowman, Sanderson, Young, Mackenzie and Cameron from Inverness, Eric Geddes was finding another crop of talented players among the ranks of the Queens Own Highlanders regiment based at Fort George.

Mike Bell and Ken Urquhart gave Geddes options in an already potent forward line. Urquhart bagged a hat-trick against Forres on 29 December. But there was concern for goalkeeper Mackenzie who was injured the previous week in a 2-1 win at Forres. The young keeper, however, recovered fully for one the club's most memorable Scottish Cup games when they met Hamilton at Douglas Park on 22 January 1963.

High drama at Hamilton

The town was buzzing with excitement as arrangements were put in place to get the legions of fans down to Lanarkshire for the Scottish Cup showdown. Nairn's last game was that 5-2 victory over Forres and confidence was high. South papers had tipped Accies as hot favourites – but Nairn were determined they were not going to be cannon fodder. And so it turned out.

The match turned into a classic, with the underdogs coming within an ace of creating a major upset. A late goal earned the home side a 1-1 draw in a storming encounter before 5,983 fans – 300 from Nairn. Gate receipts were £672.

With the freezing weather, which had kept Nairn out of action since 29 December 1962, having continued into January, nearly the entire Scottish League and Cup programme was wiped out that day. The TV cameras and radio broadcasting teams were there in force to capture every moment as an afternoon of high drama unfolded. Davy Johnston was feeling off-colour on the journey down to the match, but there was no way the talisman was going to miss out on the club's date with destiny in the national tournament:

Nairn: Mackenzie; Clark, Young; Cameron, Sanderson and Allan; Johnston, Shields, Urquhart, Clyne and Bowman.

Hamilton: McMillan; McKechnie, Holton; Strickland, Johnston, Massie; Hutton, Divers, Forsyth, Currie and Hastings.

Referee: W Syme, Glasgow.

From the kick-off it was clear to the home side that they were going to have a major hurdle to overcome if they were to figure in the ballot for the next round of the Cup. Nairn had them under the cosh for long spells with Chic Allan a powerhouse in midfield for the visitors. The craft of Clyne and Shields gave Hamilton problems all afternoon and if ever a performance could be described as a team effort this was it.

Hamilton were rocked in the 57th minute when Shields and Clyne conjured up a passing move which made space for Johnston, who took on a defender before striking a sweet left-foot drive into the corner of the net. One writer described how Johnston left Hamilton defender Holton floundering, 'and, in a twinkling, a left foot ice-defroster was in the net!'

The Nairn fans were ecstatic while the Hamilton support was dumfounded. It took Accies nearly ten minutes to recover their composure. With the clock ticking, an upset looked on the cards until an uncharacteristic mistake by Mackenzie in the Nairn goal produced the equaliser. The keeper failed to hold a lob in the 79th minute and Forsyth stabbed the ball across the line, much to the relief of the home crowd.

Hamilton had lived to battle another day and, despite Mackenzie's mistake for the goal, he had a fantastic game, making several great saves. His display was acknowledged by the Nairn fans who carried the youngster shoulder-high off the pitch at the final whistle. In today's game, where security is a priority, such a display of exuberance by fans would result in heavy penalties being meted out by the authorities.

Mackenzie in fact was just twenty years of age, and such was his performance that day he was being tipped for a move south to English football by one of the national papers which covered the tie. Vic Buckingham manager of Sheffield Wednesday, and Joe Harvey, manager at Newcastle, were said to have received glowing reports on the youngster. Mackenzie described afterwards how his feet slipped from under him as he went to catch a simple lob which led to the Hamilton goal. So delighted was one fan with his side's performance, he gave a £2 bonus to every Nairn player, a not inconsiderable sum in those days.

And so it was still all to play for with the replay scheduled for 2.15pm the following Wednesday. I confess I have little recall of events that day. All I know is I was seven years of age and my parents wouldn't allow me to take the day off school. I remember coming into class at Millbank Primary that morning and a sudden flu epidemic had mysteriously taken hold of the school population. Because I was just one of a handful of boys at their desks. Television cameras zooming in on the legions of Nairn fans, I'm told, exposed many teaching staff who had been smitten by the flu epidemic. Allegedly my own headmaster James Stark was among them and many pupils and teachers from Nairn Academy deserted their post at lunchtime to go to the match.

The *Daily Express* photographed a group of some 100 young brave fans (brave because of the possibility of repercussions on their return to school) warmly clad in their duffel coats and scarves to beat the winter chill. 'Hooray for Hookey' proclaimed the banner headlines and the paper went on to describe how 200 pupils played truant for the occasion.

Nairn Academy Rector Alex Robertson, who was attending an education committee meeting in Elgin that day, had sent a note to every class warning the pupils that it was 'just another school day and must be treated as such'. But after the defeat the rector promised there would be no action taken against the pupils who went to the game. 'We have an old Scots proverb: The more you tramp on dirt the more it spreads,' he said. 'As far as I am concerned the matter is closed. Mind you, I'm not against football – I'm a keen Nairn County supporter myself, but school must come first.' One relieved fifteen-year-old described Mr Robertson as a 'jolly good sport'.

Shops, offices and hotels closed for business so that every fan in Nairn could go to the match, and buses descended on the town from all over the north and north-east. Even a clay pigeon shoot on Cawdor Estate was cancelled. I can't turn the clock back, but missing out on this moment in the club's history is something I have always regretted. Why the education authorities never gave dispensation to all the school-kids who wanted to attend that day I'll never know.

Jimmy Phillip, a farmer from Auldearn who was a pal of Chic Allan and later played a few games for Nairn and Forres Mechanics himself, recalled what he described as a mass walk-out of senior pupils from Nairn Academy at lunchtime on the day of the match: 'We were all told that we were not allowed to go but we went anyway. And who was standing behind us at Station Park, but some of our teachers. There couldn't very well be repercussions for us, because half of the teaching staff would have had to be disciplined as well.'

Rod Clyne's view of that match was the club did themselves no favours by working tirelessly to get the pitch, which was still in the grip of frost and snow, ready for the replay. A squad of fans under the guidance of Dean of Guild and later Provost Fred Knowles used twenty braziers to defrost the bone-hard pitch. Harrows broke up some surface ice, pumps were used to clear surface water, and tons of sand were brought in and spread across parts of the pitch.

Rod's opinion was Nairn should have let nature take its course. A postponement would have given the players time to recover from their exertions on Saturday. But a pitch inspection on the Tuesday deemed it was playable. With no floodlights in those days, an early kick-off was necessary and the scene was set for another memorable 90 minutes.

The replay, however, didn't provide as tantalising a finish as the first tie at Douglas Park. But it was nonetheless a great spectacle before a crowd of 3,405 at a time when the population of the town of Nairn was probably about 6,000.

That Hamilton meant business was evident from the kick-off and they went ahead through Hastings after just one minute when his shot took a deflection off Nairn captain Sanderson. Nairn, though, did get into their stride and fought back gallantly, refusing to be steamrollered by their Scottish League opponents. Shots from Clyne and Urquhart tested McMillan in the Hamilton goal, then Johnston passed up a great chance with a shot which went agonisingly past the post.

The heavy pitch was taking its toll on the players' legs but the surface also made control difficult for the players.

Nairn suffered a crushing blow in the 74th minute when Hutton added a second for Hamilton with a close-range shot. It was a rare mistake by Nairn right-back Bobby Clark which led to the goal. He was caught in possession in the penalty area by Hastings, who fired the ball goalwards, finding Hutton at the far post to knock it into the net.

But rather than lie down, urged on by the partisan crowd, Nairn battled back and after a Chic Allan shot hit the bar and a succession of corners Nairn got a consolation goal they richly deserved through Johnston in the final minute. Their Scottish Cup dream was over. Nairn exited the competition beaten but unbowed.

One key player that day was Hamilton's centre-half Johnstone, who was a rock in the heart of their defence. Ken Urquhart, the Nairn centre-forward who was known as the Highland bull because of his bulk, switched positions with Davy Johnston, who was out on the right wing. But it was all to no avail until Johnston made the breakthrough in the last minute. By then, Nairn players were out on their feet and some of them could barely summon the strength to kick the ball, never mind raise a last-minute cavalry charge which might produce an equaliser. The teams:

Nairn: Mackenzie; Clark, Young; Cameron, Sanderson, Allan; Johnston, Shields, Urquhart, Clyne, Bowman.

Hamilton: McMillan; McKechnie, Holton; Strickland, Johnstone, Mann; Hutton, Currie, Forsyth, Hastings, Tait.

Nairn's match was the only one played in Scotland that day. It was tel-evised by Grampian TV and edited highlights were screened that night. The local paper summed up the match: 'The home side, most surely the best ever to wear Nairn colours, deserve credit for a valiant display; the committee, led by president Tom Walls, share the glory in having built a side that showed Scotland a high standard of Highland football; while the Nairn supporters are to be praised for great moral backing.'

Three days later it was back to the bread and butter of domestic foot-ball and, despite the rigours of the heavy pitch in midweek, Nairn cruised to a 3-0 win in the North Cup at Lossiemouth.

After another cold snap it was three weeks before the next game, when County served notice that they would not be intimidated by even the best the Highland League had to offer. Elgin City were 2-0 up after just seven minutes in a game at Station Park but they were sent packing with a double strike from Johnston and a further goal from Clyne.

Johnston continued to figure prominently on the scoresheet as Nairn's season continued in winning vein, and after a North Cup semi-final replay victory over Clach, Nairn were through to their first final appear-ance since 1957. Their opponents, Caley, looked down and out of the final at Kingsmills Park with two goals from Johnston and one from Clyne giving Nairn a seemingly unassailable 3-1 lead. But Caley hit back with two late goals to force a replay.

One couple who were getting married that day in Nairn found their wedding celebrations interrupted as anxious fans left the reception to find out the result. Willie Forsyth, who played for Nairn himself, married Ann Main in the Congregational Church and guests retired to the Royal Hotel for the celebrations. But with no local radio and TV coverage of the Highland League in those days, the menfolk deserted the nuptials to find out the result from fans returning from the game in Inverness.

'I can laugh at it now but I still have the wedding photos of us cutting our wedding cake and there was nobody there,' recalls Ann. 'The men had all left because they were desperate to find out how the team had got on. They were all great fans of Davy and the County and the timing of our wedding must have been a great inconvenience for them.' Willie and Ann's three sons, Billy, Craig and Jeff, like their dad, all went on to wear the colours of Nairn County.

Next up for Nairn was a visit from title challengers Rothes. Johnston scored in Nairn's 3-1 win, but at a price. He was injured and it kept him out of the the North Cup final replay the following week (16 April 1963).

It was to be a memorable day for Nairn who won 2-1 with goals from Clyne and Jackie Shields, who snatched the winner in the 74th minute. The Nairn team was given a reception fit for heroes as they arrived back with the cup for a celebration supper at the Royal Hotel to be greeted by hundreds of fans waiting outside and the Nairn Pipe Band.

Defeat at the end of April by Buckie, their first loss since November, sparked a run of poor results which ended Nairn's title hopes. But finishing third equal with 32 points showed the giant strides the club was making. Johnston's tally for the 1962-63 season was 47, and it must not be forgotten he was till just twenty years old. Clyne scored seventeen goals and Allan seven. Jackie Shields, who had bagged 22 for the season, departed in the close season, signing for Elgin City.

Elgin took the title with 45 points, aided in no small part by the scoring prowess of 'King' Willie Grant.

The expectations on Johnston the following season were high – but nobody could have anticipated the avalanche of goals to come – a total of 73, which for decades many believed to be a record in the Highland League.

Two Cups – but No Scoring Record

Apart from seasons 1938-39, when they finished fourth, and 1954-55, when they came sixth, Nairn had never really offered a serious challenge for the title since they first competed in the league after the end of the First World War in 1919-20. But the rise to prominence of the club in 1962-63 had perennial challengers Caley and Elgin anticipating a serious threat from Station Park in the following 1963-64 season.

The Wee County, as the club was known, didn't disappoint. The thrilling brand of football they produced saw home gates average 1,080. They finished the year with two trophies – the North of Scotland Cup and the Highland League Cup, and were pipped by a point for the title by Caley. This was also the season in which Johnston scored more goals than any other in his career. And it is in this chapter I will dispel the myth that he was in fact the holder of a Highland League record.

Although newspapers recorded it thus at the time, two Highland football historians have provided me with conclusive evidence that it was another Highland League star of the 1950s, Andy 'Juppy' Mitchell, to whom this honour should be rightly bestowed. When I conveyed the news to Davy's widow, Margaret, she was very disappointed and couldn't understand how such information had not been made public before now. In fact, Juppy's tally of 77 goals (52 in the league, 25 in cups) in season 1955-56 is alluded to in Bill McAllister's book *Highland Hundred*, celebrating the centenary of the Highland League. The same book features four of the Highland Leagues top strikers – Johnston, Grant, Brian Third of Peterhead, and Caley's Billy Urquhart, who also had a spell with Rangers. Johnston is credited with only 75 goals in a season, but my research shows he scored fewer, 73.

Johnston's prodigious knack of finding the net saw many top clubs casting envious eyes towards Station Park. Indeed, during the title run-in that season appears the first and only suggestion that Johnston ever wanted to quit Nairn for pastures new. This appeared in a story which ran in the *Daily Record*. Johnston himself was quoted by a reporter in April 1964 as saying he fancied a change, but only to another Highland League club because he did not fancy another crack at the big time.

What truth there was in the report, I can't say. Perhaps it was Davy realising his stock was rising, and who can blame him if he was trying to lever an extra quid or two for his pay packet – he was worth every penny. Nairn president Tom Walls sought immediately to calm the waters and assured the fans he had already spoken to Johnston and the striker had pledged to commit himself to the club for another season. In fact, Nairn were able to hold on to their talisman for another two seasons before he accepted the challenge to try his luck again in the Scottish League.

Two penalty goals by Johnston served notice that Nairn meant business in the opening game of the season against Elgin in the Highland League Cup. Alan Presslie, who was later to become a team-mate of Johnston at Caley, committed the fouls which presented the striker with two spot-kick opportunities and he grabbed them both. The 2-1 victory at Station Park, however, was much more convincing than the scoreline suggested. Another victory over Elgin, two wins against Forres, a win and defeat against Clach secured a place in the semi-final of a competition they had never previously won.

The Games Night match against Forres at Station Park which Nairn won 4-2 attracted 2,000 fans. To this day it is an evening fixture that County fans of my vintage would love to see reinstated. Nairn had ground advantage against Ross County in the semi-final but had to settle for a battling 2-2 draw. The replay to follow was a football spectacle with Johnston at his brilliant best, snatching four goals in a thrilling 7-6 victory. Ross County were behind 2-6 at one stage, and the 2,400 fans were biting their fingernails until the final whistle blew.

Johnston netted a hat-trick the following week in a 3-0 win to dump Keith, league winners only two seasons before, out of the Qualifying Cup. Then it was on to the Highland League Cup final, which was to be played at Princess Royal Park in Banff. Their opponents, Peterhead, couldn't live with Nairn that day as again Johnston ran rampant with another hat-trick as County put them to the sword with a 5-1 victory. His scoring feat in the final brought Johnston's tally to sixteen in ten matches since the start of the season. Nairn were 4-1 up at half-time and took their foot off the pedal in the second half. Johnston was carried from the field shoulder high by wildly ecstatic fans at the final whistle. But observers acknowledged it was no one-man team. Eric Geddes had assembled a side that was firing on all cylinders, with Chic Allan, 21, and Johnston, still twenty. Allan also took on the mantle of team captain, and an inspirational skipper he proved to be.

It was fitting that Nairn finally got their hands on this trophy, for it was donated to Nairn County by the wife of Angelo Morganti in memory of her late husband, a former president of the club. Also known as the Morganti Cup, Nairn handed the handsome trophy over to the Highland League and it was first contested in 1947-48. Metaphorically, Nairn set the heather on fire on the pitch that day with their brilliant first-half performance. But in a postscript to the match, it was noted that their fans nearly set the ground alight off it.

A lighted cigarette in the wooden stand was carelessly disposed of in the Nairn section of the crowd. It wedged in a crack and smoke was pouring from the stand as fans leapt to cheer Leighton's opening goal for Nairn. A member of the Nairn committee that day was Bob Gordon, who like his son had a career as sub-officer in the fire service. Bob grabbed a pail of water and within seconds had the outbreak under control, allowing fans to return to their seats. It may have seemed funny at the time, but a fire in 1985 at Bradford City's Valley Parade stadium cost 56 lives. That disaster would be the catalyst for smoking bans in grounds and a complete review of materials used in the construction of sporting stadiums.

More than 1,000 fans and the Nairn Pipe Band stopped traffic in the High Street in Nairn to welcome the returning heroes home after their cup victory. Tommy Sanderson and Johnston held the glittering prize aloft and at the post-match dinner at the Royal Hotel all were congratulated on their efforts. But Sanderson singled out Johnston for special mention, noting he had scored ten goals in the past three games.

Unsurprisingly there was talk again of clubs knocking on the Nairn president's door for permission to speak to Johnston. Dundee and Tommy Pearson's Aberdeen both had made official approaches but they were rebuffed by the player himself who said he was perfectly happy to play for his home-town team – 'They're a grand lot of chaps,' he added. For the record, the Nairn team in the final was: Mackenzie; Clark, Young; Cameron, Sanderson, Chisholm; Leighton, Robertson, Johnston, Mair, Bowman.

Following their heroic League Cup performance, Nairn supporters were looking forward to the following week's encounter with Elgin in the Qualifying Cup. The semi-finalists of this competition qualified for the national Scottish Cup and after their memorable trip to Hamilton the previous year the fans had the appetite for more. But it was not to be. Johnston was on the scoresheet again but they crashed to a 1-3 defeat at Elgin, with disgruntled fans blaming the wrong team selection for the defeat.

A Johnston double kick-started Nairn's challenge for the title when they played their first league game of the season on 28 September against Rothes, but the following week they only managed a 4-4 draw with Peterhead after leading 4-1 with fifteen minutes to go – a squandered point that was to prove very costly. Opposition defences clearly were being given a torrid time by Johnston, who had racked up 39 goals in 22 games by the end of November. The tally was up to 47 before the year was out (matching his total for the previous season). But Elgin followed up their earlier Qualifying Cup win with victories in the league both at home and away against Nairn in December and January.

In December 1963, Nairn made one of their best ever signings when they secured the services of Andy Cadenhead from St Johnstone. The 26-year-old full-back had been five seasons at Pittodrie with Aberdeen and played 55 first-team matches before moving on to Muirton Park.

A researcher at the Rowatt Institute in Aberdeen, Cadenhead was released by the Perth club when they opted to go full-time. He went on to become a stalwart in the defence at Station Park and a great favourite with the fans. He eventually became team captain and moved from full-back to centre-half where he was a commanding presence. He was a key player in the Nairn side which won the Qualifying Cup final in 1968-69 over two legs against Fraserburgh. I remember vividly marching down Nairn High Street with the legions of fans celebrating after an uninspiring 1-1 draw in the second leg at Station Park secured the trophy for the first and only time by a Nairn side. Nairn had already beaten Fraserburgh 3-1 in a much more entertaining first leg at Bellslea.

A 1-5 home defeat against Caley dented morale in January 1964, when St Johnstone underlined their ambitions by becoming the latest club to make overtures for Johnston's signature – the response was entirely predictable. Nairn, though, had the measure of Caley and Elgin in February when they progressed to the North Cup final with a 4-3 win at Telford Street and a narrow 1-0 win at Borough Briggs. Rothes put a dent in their title hopes with a 4-2 victory at Station Park on 15 February, but Nairn bounced back the following week with a 5-0 trouncing of Ross County.

And it is here that my own research uncovered an error which, once made, was going to be perpetuated for decades as fans argued what indeed was Johnston's record goals tally for that season. I use the term 'record' advisedly because although it was not a Highland League record it certainly was a club record. Totals of 72 and 75 have been bandied about over the years and the conclusion of the local paper was the figure of 72. But my predecessor at the *Nairnshire Telegraph*, Alex Laing, who had a passion for sporting statistics, recorded Johnston's tally after two goals in a 6-1 win at Fraserburgh on 11 January 1964 at 51 goals. That is a figure I concur with, as you will see from the scoring chart further on in this chapter.

However, in subsequent matches before the game with Ross County on 22 February, Johnston's scoring record was this: Nairn 1, Caley 5 (0); Nairn 6, Keith 0 (3); Caley 3, Nairn 4 (2); Nairn 3, Golspie 0 (2); Nairn 2, Rothes 4 (0). This brought his total up to 58. The coverage in the *Nairnshire* of the match against Ross County acknowledges that Johnston scored four goals in the last twenty minutes of that match, but another snippet added that his goal tally was now 61 when it should have been 62.

The only explanation, I suspect, for this uncharacteristic error by Alex, who was one of the most highly respected journalists in the north of Scotland, is that he glanced at the match report and extracted the goalscorers which were highlighted in capital letters. In the match report of the Ross County game, Johnston's name figured in capitals only three times. But the paragraph about his second goal in 82 minutes continued into his third goal two minutes later. It is an assumption on my part that this is how the mistake occurred. But having been made, it was perpetuated right through to end of the season.

I hasten to add it gives me no pleasure to raise this issue because Alex nurtured me in my early years as a cub reporter and he instilled in me a sense of fairness, accuracy and propriety I hope I have maintained in this profession for nearly four decades. He was a wonderful person who served the *Nairnshire Telegraph* loyally for over 50 years. He acted as a correspondent for all the national daily papers, who held him in the highest esteem.

Alex Laing was disabled and never enjoyed the best of health. I have no doubt that, had it not been so, he would have moved south to a distinguished career with the national dailies. When he felt he was no longer able to sit in the stand during the long cold winter months providing commentary for the readers of the *Nairnshire*, that mantle was taken on by David Bain, a lifelong fan and fellow *Nairnshire Telegraph* employee. When I joined the staff of the paper in 1971 I took over the duties of providing the match reports, which I continued to do until I left the paper in 1997.

Into the month of March 1964, and the team was back in the final of the North of Scotland Cup, with Clach providing the opposition. Johnston, the hat-trick hero of the Highland League Cup final, took centre stage again with both goals in a 2-1 North Cup win at Telford Street before 2,000 fans to complete the first cup double in the club's history. Johnston's goals in the final both came in the opening five minutes of the second half. Both were described as brilliantly executed, with the tireless Allan aided and abetted by Cameron and Bowman, providers in chief. There were seven minutes remaining when Rowan, who finished the season as the Highland League's second top scorer behind Johnston, snatched a consolation goal for Clach.

At the celebrations which followed in Nairn, Rod Clyne, who played no small part in the Nairn victory, got a special cheer from the crowd when he appeared as the big drummer with the pipe band. I don't know if Rod was ever a drummer, but a charismatic figure he certainly was, with a great sense of fun and zest for life.

The festivities continued and the players paid tribute to their captain Chic Allan by taking the trophy out to his home village of Auldearn, where another large crowd had assembled to honour Nairn County's achievement.

The entire Nairn team visited Chic's parents, Jimmy and Mary Allan, in their home at 1 County Cottages. Chic's eldest sister, Kathleen Gemmell, recalled her mother had baked a batch of scones which the players tucked into: 'Some of them even wrote letters to my mother thanking her and said they were the best scones they had ever tasted.'

Kathleen's late husband John was in the RAF and regularly went to watch County when he was stationed at Kinloss: 'When we were posted abroad mum and dad kept us in touch by sending us copies of the *Sunday Post* and *Football Times*. Chic had a spell too with Hearts [very brief, he never played]. They got him a job at the infirmary in Edinburgh but like Davy he didn't like the big city and he came home too.' Nine years later the shocked community would be mourning Chic's tragic passing. But that cup celebration must have been special for Chic and his family.

After their second cup success, victories over Buckie, Deveronvale and Brora sustained Nairn's title challenge. But they needed victory, and nothing less would do, when they were to take on the might of Caley on their home turf on 2 May at Telford Street to keep that title dream alive. It was Caley's last game of the season. A draw would take them on to 44 points and out of reach. Nairn were on 40 points with two games to go. The atmosphere was highly charged with 3,000 fans inside the ground. Exchanges were fast and furious at both ends and the teams contrived to serve up one of the most exciting no-scoring draws ever.

Caley: J Smith; Glennie, Ross; Patience, Davidson, Duchart; H Smith, McInnes, Reid, Mackenzie, Stephen.

Nairn: Mackenzie; Cadenhead, Young; Cameron, Sanderson, Allan; Matheson, Clyne, Johnston, Mair, Bowman.

There were thrills galore at both ends with Caley the early aggressors, with one shot coming off the Nairn bar. An Alex Bowman shot was cleared off the Caley line, and as Nairn threw caution to the wind in the final stages a Johnston effort came agonisingly off the base of the Caley post. Had it gone in, the title would have been Nairn's but it was not be. A draw was a fair result and the title was Caley's.

Johnston completed his goal-haul the following week with two more in a 3-1 win over Fraserburgh, which concluded a record-breaking season in more ways than one for the County faithful. They had finished in their highest league position ever, completed a cup double, and their talisman Johnston had set what many believed was a Highland League record, beating Willie Grant's tally of 65 in 1960-61 with Elgin City.

Caley finished the season on 44 points, Nairn on 43. In this, his most prolific year in the Highland League, Johnston scored 23 cup and 50 league goals, including ten penalties. In one match he scored five goals, in three matches four, three hat-tricks and on eighteen occasions he scored twice. An ever-present in the 46 games played that season, he only failed to find the net in nine of them. Other top scorers were Clyne twelve, Ronnie Mair, a winger signed at the start of the season from Lossie, had eleven goals and Bowman ten.

Needless to say, it was a very upbeat annual meeting with a surplus of £560 reported, compared to the £47 deficit a few seasons before. Gates improved by an average of 60 to 1,080 – a record for the club. All the players were congratulated and the chairman, Tom Walls, congratulated Chic Allan for his inspirational leadership of the team.

It was intended to present Johnston with a gift to mark his goal-scoring achievement but he preferred not to attend – a further indication of how this unassuming individual avoided the limelight.

Here is a timeline of the phenomenal goalscoring achievement of Davy Johnston in season 1963-64. Abbreviations: Highland League Cup (HLC), North of Scotland Cup (NOSC), Highland League (HL), Qualifying Cup (QC), Inverness Cup (IC).

10 August 1963 HLC Nairn 2, Elgin City 1 (2 goals).

14 August 1963 HLC Clach 3, Nairn 0.

17 August 1963 HLC Nairn 4, Forres Mechs 2 (1 goal).

22 August 1963 HLC HLC Nairn 3, Clach 0.

24 August 1963 HLC Forres Mechs 3, Nairn 4 (1 goal).

27 August 1963 HLC Elgin City 0, Nairn 1 (1 goal).

31 August 1963 HLC (Semi-final) Nairn 2, Ross C 2 (1 goal).

4 September 1963 HLC (Semi-final replay) Ross C 6, Nairn 7 (4 goals).

7 September 1963 QC Nairn 3, Keith 0 (3 goals).

14 September 1963 HLC Final at Banff Nairn 5, Peterhead 1 (3 goals).

21 September 1963 QC Elgin City 3, Nairn 1 (1 goal).

28 September 1963 HL Nairn 4, Rothes 2 (2 goals).

5 October 1963 HL Peterhead 4, Nairn 4 (2 goals).

12 October 1963 HL Nairn 5, Deveronvale 1 (2 goals).

19 October 1963 HL Ross County 1, Nairn 2 (2 goals).

26 October 1963 HL Nairn 2, Lossiemouth 2 (2 goals).

2 November 1963 HL Keith 3, Nairn County 6 (1 goal).

9 November 1963 HL Clach 1, Nairn 1 (1 goal).

13 November 1963 IC Caley 3, Nairn 2 (2 goals).

16 November 1963 HL Nairn 2, Peterhead 1 (1 goal).

23 November 1963 HL Buckie 4, Nairn 2 (2 goals).

30 November 1963 HL Nairn 6, Brora 0 (5 goals).

7 December 1963 HL Elgin 4, Nairn 3 (2 goals).

14 December 1963 HL Inverness Thistle 3, Nairn 4 (2 goals).

28 December 1963 HL Forres Mechs 2, Nairn 5 (4 goals).

2 January 1964 HL Nairn 3, Forres Mechs 0 (2 goals).

4 January 1964 HL Nairn 1, Elgin City 3.

11 January 1964 HL Fraserburgh 1, Nairn 6 (2 goals).

18 January 1964 HL Nairn 1, Caley 5.

25 January 1964 HL Nairn 6, Keith 0 (3 goals).

1 February 1964 NOSC Caley 3, Nairn 4 (2 goals).

8 February 1964 NOSC Nairn 3, Golspie 0 (2 goals).

15 February 1964 HL Nairn 2, Rothes 4.

22 February 1964 HL Nairn 5, Ross County 0 (4 goals).

29 February 1964 NOSC Semi-final Elgin City 0, Nairn 1.

7 March 1964 HL Huntly 1, Nairn 0.

14 March 1964 HL Nairn 4, Inverness Thistle 1 (1 goal).

22 March 1964 NOSC final at Telford Street Nairn 2, Clach 1 (2 goals).

28 March 1964 HL Lossiemouth 2, Nairn 1.

4 April 1964 HL Nairn 2, Huntly 1 (1 goal).

14 April 1964 HL Nairn 2 Clach 0 (1 goal).

18 April 1964 HL Nairn 4, Buckie Thistle 3 (2 goals).

22 April 1964 HL Deveronvale 1, Nairn 2.

25 April 1964 HL Brora 2, Nairn 3 (2 goals).

2 May 1964 HL Caley 0, Nairn 0.

9 May 1964 HL Nairn 3, Fraserburgh 1 (2 goals). Total 73.

For clarification that Davy had been accredited with the Highland League scoring record, I found many references to this in the media. Any visitors to the Highland Football Academy at Dingwall will see a picture of Davy on the wall of fame. Below his photograph there is an inscription which attests to Davy holding the record with 75 goals – another inaccuracy I have previously alluded to. His record is also mentioned in Bill McAllister's book *Highland Hundred* published in 1993.

I confess I am puzzled and can offer no answer to the false legend that it was Johnston who held the scoring record.

Andy 'Juppy' Mitchell scored 52 league goals and was credited with a further 25 cup goals, having played 45 games for Inverness Thistle. In 1955-56, his total of 77 goals therefore beats Davy's total by four. It's not the only record Mitchell holds, for on 6 September 1952, while playing for Caley, he scored all ten goals in his team's 10-3 win over Fraserburgh. It was claimed his team-mates, sensing history was in the making, dribbled round the keeper and left Mitchell to finish off some.

A breakdown of Mitchell's record was compiled by Highland League historians Bob Weir of Elgin and Ian Davidson, using copies of *The Football Times*, *Nairnshire Telegraph*, *Green Final*, *Inverness Courier*, *Northern Scot* and *Banffshire Advertiser* for their research. Below are Mitchell's scoring achievements and games played that season, confirmed through newspaper accounts after Juppy's scoring feat was drawn to my attention.

Mitchell missed one game that season, against Clach played on 20 April, and one league match against Ross County was not played. His team finished third in the league on 38 points, having scored 108 goals – sixteen more than league champions Elgin, who beat Buckie Thistle 3-2 in a play-off after the clubs finished joint top on 45 points. Another fascinating part of this tale was Juppy played two league games for Thistle in one day. This was on the last Saturday of this season, in which he scored five goals in total. On the afternoon of 12 May 1956, Thistle beat Peterhead 5-1, with Juppy scoring two goals. And in the evening they defeated Lossiemouth 4-0, with Juppy scoring a hat-trick. What a testimony to the fitness of these part-time footballers, playing two games in one day.

Bob Weir explained: 'In those days the Scottish Football Association wouldn't give the Highland League extensions to the season, so teams moved heaven and earth to get their programmes completed. Sometimes they simply couldn't fit all the games in.

'Lossie in fact played Ross County in the afternoon on the same Saturday they met Thistle in the evening. Thistle were due to play another game against Ross County but that was never fulfilled. The season before, 1954-55, no one won the league because the season was never completed.'

Here follows 'Juppy' Mitchell's complete scoring record for 1955-56. Abbreviations: Highland League Cup (HLC), North of Scotland Cup (NOSC), Highland League (HL), Scottish Supplementary Cup (SSC), SC Scottish Cup, Inverness Cup (IC).

13 August 1955 HLC Thistle 0, Caley 2.
17 August 1955 HLC Thistle 2, Clach 2.
20 August 1955 HLC Thistle 6, Ross County 2 (4 goals).
24 August 1955 HLC Ross County 3, Thistle 9 (2 goals).
27 August 1955 HLC Thistle 5, Clach 0 (2 goals).
31 August 1955 HLC Thistle 3, Caley 2 (1 goal).
3 September 1955 HLC Buckie Thistle 1, Thistle 1 (1 goal).
10 September 1955 SC Edinburgh University 0, Thistle 7 (3 goals).
14 September 1955 HLC Thistle 4, Buckie Thistle 7 (2 goals).
24 September 1955 SC Thistle 5, Buckie Thistle 2 (2 goals).
1 October 1955 HL Thistle 6, Deveronvale (5 goals).
8 October 1955 SC Thistle 1, Peebles Rovers 1.
15 October 1955 SC Peebles Rovers 2, Thistle 1.
22 October 1955 HL Thistle 4, Huntly 2.
29 October 1955 HL Thistle 3, Fraserburgh 4 (2 goals).

5 November 1955 HL Thistle 7, Rothes 1 (3 goals).

12 November 1955 HL Lossiemouth 3, Thistle 1 (1 goal).

19 November 1955 HL Deveronvale 2, Thistle 5 (4 goals).

26 November 1955 HL Thistle 6, Forres Mechanics 3 (2 goals).

3 December 1955 HL Ross County 4, Thistle 5.

10 December 1955 HL Thistle 3, Keith 2 (2 goals).

17 December 1955 HL Elgin City 2, Thistle 0.

24 December 1955 HL Rothes1, Thistle 5 (2 goals).

31 December 1955 HL Caley 4, Thistle 3 (3 goals).

2 January 1956 HL Thistle 0, Clach 3.

7 January 1956 HL Thistle 8, Elgin City 1 (5 goals).

14 January 1956 HL Buckie Thistle 1, Thistle 0.

21 January 1956 HL Forres Mechanics 3, Thistle (2 goals).

28 January 1956 NSC Forres Mechanics 3, Thistle 0.

4 February 1956 HL Huntly 3, Thistle 1.

11 February 1956 HL Keith 2, Thistle 6 (3 goals).

18 February 1956 HL Thistle 11, Nairn County 0 (4 goals).

25 February 1956 HL Nairn County 3, Thistle 6 (3 goals).

3 March 1956 SSC Thistle 2, Rothes 1.

17 March 1956 SSC Thistle 3, Aberdeen University 2 (2 goals).

24 March 1956 HL Peterhead 3, Thistle 6 (3 goals).

31 March 1956 SSC Thistle 5, Keith 0 (4 goals).

7 April 1956 HL Fraserburgh 1, Thistle 4 (2 goals).

19 April 1956 SSC Thistle 2, Buckie Thistle 1.

25 April 1956 SSC Nairn County 0, Thistle 1.

28 April 1956 SSC Thistle 4, Nairn County 2 (2 goals).

5 May 1956 HL Thistle 1, Buckie Thistle 2.

9 May 1956 HL Thistle 2, Caley 1 Caley (1 goal).

12 May 1956 (afternoon) HL Thistle 5, Peterhead 1 (2 goals).

12 May 1956 (evening) HL Thistle 4, Lossiemouth 0 (3 goals). Total 77.

Mitchell died at the tragically young age of 39 after suffering a heart attack in his car in Telford Street on 29 March 1968. At the height of his scoring prowess he was being courted by clubs from the south and received a signing offer from Celtic. But communications with the north of Scotland were not like they are today and Glasgow seemed a long way from home. Andy, repelled all offers to the delight of north fans, but his career was brought to an end by a knee injury. Following his death, his friends in football in the north honoured him with a memorial match against Celtic and over £2,000 was raised for his widow and their young son.

That testimonial was a foretaste of things to come, as a select team of Inverness Thistle and Inverness Caley lined up against a strong Celtic side on Saturday, 11 May 1968 at Telford Street. The two clubs later amalgamated to become Inverness Caley-Thistle and of course have made a terrific impact since their admission to the Scottish League. Celtic's line-up that night included most of the Lisbon Lions and 10,000 fans turned out to pay their own tribute to Andy. Celtic won the friendly match 6-1. The Glasgow giants took the lead after three minutes through Willie Wallace and, although Hugh Lazenby equalised for the select, Celtic finished runaway winners with a Gemmell penalty and Bobby Murdoch putting them 3-1 in front at the interval. Murdoch, Gemmell (with another penalty) and Bobby Lennox completed the scoring in the second half. The teams for Juppy's memorial match were:

Inverness select: Connell (Caley); Bennett (Caley), Gitsam (Thistle); Sutherland (Thistle), Presslie (Caley), Macinnes (Caley); T Fraser (Thistle), Allan (Caley), Grant (Thistle), Lazenby (Thistle), F Neild (Caley); reserves R Fraser (Thistle), Noble (Caley).

Celtic: Fallon; Gemmell, O'Neil; Murdoch, McNeill, Brogan; Johnstone, Gallagher, Wallace, Lennox, Hughes; subs Wraith and Hay.

Referee: Ward Balfour, Inverness.

A Broken Nose – a Title Lost

The County had just enjoyed their most successful season ever – two cups, a new club goalscoring record by Johnston, and what was thought by many to be a Highland League record. But failing at the final hurdle in the championship was a bitter pill to swallow. Would 1964-65 be their year to finally capture that elusive title? Sadly not. And there are some who would argue that a freak injury to Johnston was to cost them the championship.

Despite again taking the championship right to the wire, Nairn were again pipped for the title by just one point – this time by their neighbours from Moray, Elgin City. Defeats in the Highland League Cup and Inverness Cup finals meant Nairn finished runners-up in three competitions. If ever there was a season to reflect ruefully 'what might have been', this was it.

A defeat by Caley saw them lose their grip of the North Cup, and any aspirations of a Scottish Cup run were snuffed out by Keith in an extraordinary match when Nairn crashed to a 4-10 defeat at Station Park. But it was an eventful year for many other reasons. Chic Allan, who was blossoming in his role as team captain, emerged as a lethal goalscorer in his own right. In fact his season's haul of 44 was one more than Johnston, who missed six games through a broken nose. He later cited this as an inhibiting factor in his ability to perform at the highest level, which contributed to his quitting Aberdeen.

I suspect, however, events off the field during, and at the end of, this season were later to influence Johnston's decision to ultimately take the plunge and move to Pittodrie in 1966. But more about that later.

It is significant that throughout his Nairn career, even when he was not on the scoresheet, Johnston's performances never failed to elicit praise – even in defeat. His value to the team was not just as a goal-grabber. He was inspirational in every aspect of his play. When he wasn't putting the ball in the back of the net, his ability to get away from markers, find space, precision passing and tremendous pace, vision and awareness of what was going on around him, created a package that opposition defences were seldom able to find an answer to.

Nairn couldn't have hoped for a better start to the 1964-65 campaign. By the end of August they were through to the final of the Highland League Cup and Johnston already had eleven goals to his credit.

After a tentative 3-2 away win in this competition against Thistle at Kingsmills, Nairn's resolve would undoubtedly be tested by perennial challengers Elgin at Borough Briggs. But two goals from Johnston secured the points with a 2-0 victory. Forres spoiled the Games Night celebrations with a 4-3 win at Nairn, but County's challenge in their League Cup section was put back on track the following week with an 11-0 thumping of a young Thistle side, Johnston bagging five goals. A 4-2 draw at Mosset Park in the return against Forres, followed by a 3-3 draw with Elgin at Nairn, gave them nine points from six games and their semi-final slot was secured.

A new striker, Dave Beveridge, was scoring for County, and four goals from him and one from Bowman gave Nairn a comfortable passage through to the final with a 5-1 win over Deveronvale.

Their league campaign got off to a good start with a 4-3 home win against Fraserburgh, but the League Cup final was to prove a disappointing day out for the Nairn fans. A crowd of 3,700 watched Keith take the handsome silverware in a 1-0 victory, the goal coming from Whytock on 74 minutes. A late header from Maclennan off a Johnston cross was the most serious threat posed by Nairn, but his effort was saved and the League Cup would not be returning to the Station Park boardroom.

Nairn: Mackenzie; Cadenhead, Young; Cameron, Sanderson, Allan; Maclennan, Beveridge, Johnston, Mair, Bowman.

With no Kessock, Cromarty or Dornoch bridges in those days, a draw against Wick in the Qualifying Cup was always a daunting journey. Wick were not members of the Highland League but qualified for both the North of Scotland and Qualifying Cups.

Nairn were paired with the Scorries for a first round Qualifying Cup tie on 19 September but the game was a wash-out, the referee calling it off at the last minute – a 290-mile round-trip for nothing. Nairn returned the following week and did the business 4-3, but not without a scare. The lads from Caithness were 3-1 up but Nairn recovered and a Johnston double and goals from Beveridge and Maclennan took them through to the next round.

Keith, however, were back to haunt Nairn again and dumped them out of the competition in the next round with a 4-10 hammering at Station Park.

The league provided some respite after their early season cup disappointments, and a 3-2 win at Lossie, a 5-3 victory against Thistle at Kingsmills, and a 6-3 home win over Vale at Nairn gave County full points from their first four games.

But now Chic Allan was beginning to find the net as regularly as Johnston. The rumour-mill had it that Nairn were scouting for another forward. This bemused local fans who were watching Johnston and Allan scoring for fun – the terracing pundits were more concerned about the number of goals being conceded.

Nairn continued their unbeaten run in the league into November but an injury to Johnston in a game against Inverness Thistle clearly impeded their momentum. Thirty minutes into the match the Nairn centre clashed in the air with Thistle centre-half Roy Fraser who was attempting to clear the ball with his head.

There was no ill-intent on Fraser's part. It was just a good honest challenge, but Johnston needed six stitches to his fractured nose. He was allowed home from hospital but had to go for an x-ray the following day. It was this injury Johnston later claimed was causing him respiratory problems when he later quit the Dons. Fraser for his part received a cut to his head but resumed play after treatment in the dressing room. Freddie Neild had given Thistle the lead after twenty minutes but eight minutes after Davy left the field Maclennan snatched an equaliser for Nairn.

There were no substitutes in those days and Nairn had to soldier on with ten men. To their credit, Nairn battled to a man and their captain Allan scored a brilliant solo effort in the 81st minute to secure the points. The following Wednesday Nairn squeezed through to the final of the

Inverness Cup with a 1-0 win against Clach. With the final against Ross County scheduled for the following Wednesday, the sides had a dress rehearsal in the league on Saturday. Even with the absence of Johnston through injury, what happened at Victoria Park that day was not in anyone's script. Tommy Ross, the Dingwall outside-right, ran amok, scoring seven goals in an 8-1 annihilation of Nairn.

The omens were not good for the cup final and so it proved. Nairn were 2-5 down at one stage and battled back to 4-5. But the Dingwall side held sway and finished 7-5 victors. Nairn's erratic form continued with a league defeat against Elgin and a draw with Huntly. A 3-2 win over Keith gave them a modicum of revenge for the damage the Kynoch Park side had done in the League and Qualifying Cups.

After missing six games, Johnston returned to the fold on Boxing Day and resumed his scoring alliance with Allan as they both bagged hat-tricks in a 6-2 win at Forres. A happy festive season was made complete with a 4-2 win in the return match against Forres.

Another two points from a 2-0 win on 9 January 1965 at Deveronvale saw Nairn well placed for their title challenge. They were sitting in third place with 23 points from fifteen games. Caley were one point ahead on the same number of games and Ross County were on top with 26 points but having played eighteen games.

That week the earlier rumours that Nairn had been in the market for another forward were confirmed when they signed Billy Smith. Having had experience with Darlington in the English League, Smith, a skilful inside-forward, was to prove a shrewd acquisition. Perhaps the Nairn committee were already aware that their captain Allan had ambitions and might move on and they wanted to prepare for that eventuality. If so, their suspicions were well founded because Chic did leave Nairn at the end of that season. But Aberdeen-based Smith became an automatic choice after his arrival at Nairn and following Allan's departure he forged a deadly striking partnership with Johnston. Smith was later to play his part in Nairn's successful Qualifying Cup campaign of 1968-69. Now, he was immediately pitched into the side and scored on his home debut – a 4-1 win over Peterhead.

Attendances in those days, of course, were tremendous. Caley pulled in 4,500 for a Scottish Cup-tie with Raith at Telford Street in January 1965, and the following month, having beaten Rovers 2-1, there was a crowd of 6,500 to see Third Lanark beat them 5-1 at Cathkin Park. The Thirds sadly folded in 1967.

Five league points were dropped during Johnston's enforced absence – his broken nose, it might be argued, would cost them the title. His return, however, steadied the ship and a further 4-2 win at home against Brora left them lying third in the table with 27 points from eighteen games. Defeats by Keith and Buckie in February were followed by a North Cup exit to Caley but Nairn were to get back on song and, with Allan and Johnston hitting the net with consummate regularity, they won five of their next six league games.

A 3-2 win over Buckie on 17 April saw them go joint top of the league with Ross County on 37 points. But Ross had played 28 games, three more than Nairn. However, lurking ominously in third place on 26 points with a game in hand over Nairn were Elgin. The race for the title was reaching fever pitch. Nairn came from two goals down to beat a fighting Clach side 3-2 at Grant Street, thanks to an Allan hat-trick, to set themselves up for a showdown on 24 April with Elgin at Borough Briggs.

This was to be described as the team's 'finest hour' when they overcame the mighty Elgin 4-2 to edge one point in front on 43 points from 28 games with only two fixtures each remaining. Johnston and Allan, described as 'invaluable goal-snapping opportunists', scored two apiece. Nairn fans felt they should have been four up but there were no goals by half-time. Johnston, though, had been giving the Elgin defence an uncomfortable afternoon. He finally made the breakthrough on 50 minutes from a free-kick after he was brought down on the edge of the box. With the City defence anticipating a typical Johnston rocket, he delicately flighted a looping ball over the wall and into the net beyond Adrian Connell's reach – a goal that David Beckham would have been proud of. It was just another example of the fantastic array of skills Johnston had in his armoury. Three minutes later Johnston set Allan up for Nairn's second. Stephen pulled one back for Elgin but Nairn were in no mood for lying down and further goals from Johnston and Allan put them out of Elgin's reach, although a late goal from McIntosh gave the home side a second consolation goal.

Now in pole position, Nairn needed wins from their last two games to claim that elusive title. But they hadn't bargained for the battling qualities of Clach. Nairn were dumped 1-4 by the Lilywhites at Station Park.

Richard Konczak, later to become the first Nairn keeper to taste the sweet success of winning a league championship, was at the match. I still meet Richard regularly on the terracing at Station Park. He has a deep affection for the club he served so well. When we were both pupils at Nairn Academy, Richard was already being groomed as Kenny Mackenzie's successor. Such was his dedication, I remember he would fly past me every morning, lunch-time and at the end of the school day as he used the journey between his home at Boath Park and the academy as a training run. He has a prodigious memory of events in this era, although he was but a lad of ten, and he tells me of the deep despair he felt at the final whistle of this match.

Not even Nairn's 2-1 win against Caley in the last game of the season could deny Elgin, who took full points from their final two games. Nairn fans were inconsolable as the title once again eluded them by the narrowest of margins – one point. Elgin finished on 46 and Nairn on 45 and, to add to Nairn's woes, Allan's immediate departure was confirmed as he signed a contract with Caley. Allan finished the season with 44 goals and Johnston 43. Elgin's Willie Grant was recrowned the goal king of the Highland League with 45.

I mentioned earlier that there were probably a combination of factors that season which ultimately would influence Johnston's departure to the Dons the following year. Not least of those was the loss of his stablemate Allan to Caley. Allan's departure had broken up a formidable partnership forged in their schooldays which had blossomed on Davy's return from Hearts. The loss, too, of Tommy Sanderson to Elgin that close season and Alex Bowman to pastures new was another indication that the great side that had been assembled by Eric Geddes could be breaking up. Another factor, which probably had gone unnoticed, was the arrival in March 1965 of Eddie Turnbull at Aberdeen.

Turnbull showed he meant business by releasing seventeen players from Pittodrie. They had to be replaced, and in November he followed the path of his predecessor Tommy Pearson and came knocking at Nairn's door enquiring about Johnston. But Turnbull was greeted with the same response so many other clubs had received. Johnston was happy at Nairn. A year later though, Turnbull's persistence would pay off and, using all his powers of persuasion, he finally lured the master goal-grabber away from his comfort zone at Nairn.

A Tiger in the Tank

An advertising slogan by petrol giants Esso to put a tiger in your tank was how Davy Johnston's high-octane start to 1965-66 season was described. Johnston was the tiger in the tank with four goals as Nairn quickly got into top gear, beating Forres 6-4 at Station Park in the Highland League Cup.

The following week Nairn visited Telford Street and I wonder perhaps if Chic Allan finished his afternoon's work with mixed feelings. He certainly gave no quarter and asked none as he put his old club to the sword with a devastating double hat-trick. The match finished 10-4 in Caley's favour but reports of the match suggest Nairn had as many chances and the final scoreline didn't truly reflect the balance of play.

Auldearn farmer Jimmy Phillip was standing on the terracing that day beside Nairn policeman Bert Diack. Bert was a likable old style bobby who was well known in the community. He loved his football and with his dry sense of humour was prone to come out with some lovely one-liners. Jimmy recalls, as the goals came raining in, the despairing Bert buried his head in his hands and cried : 'Oh Chic, how could you do that to Nairn?' How indeed?

Goalkeeper Kenny Mackenzie, who had been holding out for a better deal, returned to the Nairn side for the following game against Forres Mechanics. But even Kenny's presence couldn't contain the lively Can-Cans who trounced Nairn 7-3. Nairn were 5-1 up the following week against Caley but the Blues battled back to 5-5 in an unforgettable match. In the first four games of the season Nairn had scored twenty goals in the Highland League Cup, but accrued only three points because they had conceded 24 – crowds had seen an average of eleven goals a game – no wonder gates in the Highland League in those days averaged over 1,000.

A 1-3 defeat at Elgin followed, and home wins over City and Caley were not enough to see Nairn through to the knock-out stages of the competition.

Victory over Keith, then a loss at Dingwall, saw a stuttering start to the league, and a Qualifying Cup defeat after a second replay by Elgin before 2,500 fans provided an uninspiring start to the new season.

By the end of the year it was clear the exodus of talent from Station Park had taken its toll. Nairn had six league wins and five defeats – certainly not the kind of form demanded by sides with title aspirations. The one bright spot was Johnston still hadn't lost his knack for scoring and had racked up another 21 goals as 1966 beckoned.

The New Year began in brighter fashion with five league wins out of six dragging Nairn up the table. Then in February the North of Scotland Football Association voted by six votes to three to support the introduction of substitutes, when asked for their views by the national governing body, the SFA. But it would take several more years before the new law would be introduced.

The signs were that Nairn were beginning to gel after the upheaval of the previous summer and indeed they were rewarded with a North of Scotland Cup final appearance against Caley. I was eleven years of age and this was to be my first experience of watching Nairn in a major final. My father took me to Clach's Grant Street Park where we watched a thrilling encounter before 3,000 spectators which left the sides dead-locked at 4-4 after a nerve-jangling 90 minutes.

It was back to Grant Street for a re-run the following week and Nairn triumphed 3-2 after extra-time – their third North Cup win in four seasons. Caley had had a midweek match, while Nairn were fully rested. Nairn finished worthy winners, although two of the Nairn goals were credited to Caley defenders. Billy Smith, however, could lay claim to the first after eleven minutes. His artistry, weaving through a crowded goal-mouth, threw the Caley defence into all-out panic. He drew the goal-keeper nicely and was just about to place his shot when a Caley boot came flying in. But what was meant to be a saving tackle was a costly intervention. Instead of clearing the ball, the defender knocked it into his own net.

Johnston then sent a blistering free-kick crashing against the bar as play ranged from end to end. Stephen equalised for Caley in the 22nd minute but there was no denying Smith, who grabbed Nairn's second after good lead-up play by midfield maestro Jim Cameron in the 75th minute. Andy Kerr levelled the game for Caley and the match went to extra-time. Five minutes from the end, Caley's keeper, in an attempt to clear, struck the ball against Alan Presslie and the ball rebounded into the net for the winning goal. Presslie was a giant in the Caley defence of that era and it must have been a crushing blow for him personally. But it was an irony that it should take an own-goal to decide a final between two great sides after 210 minutes of thrilling football.

In the Nairn line-up that day was sixteen-year-old Nairn Academy pupil David 'Pop' Ross. Rodwill Clyne had lured him to train with Caley reserves, but Nairn stepped in at the eleventh hour to sign him. Dave, although eight years Johnston's junior, grew up with him on the same housing estate. He went on to Aberdeen University and secured a degree in teaching and taught at Harlaw Academy and Bankhead Academy. He had a glittering Highland League career with Ross County, Huntly, and Peterhead, where he won every honour except the league title. He also had a spell with Deveronvale when Jim Leighton was emerging as a promising young keeper. Here are the full teams:

Caley: J Smith; Presslie, Hogg; Patience, Mair, Allan; H Smith, Cumming, Kerr, McInnes, Stephen.

Nairn: Mackenzie; Cadenhead, Young, Cameron, Nairn, Grant; Ross, Smith, Johnston, Godsman, Murray.

For me, this match was a moment to treasure and years later I was to take two of my own sons, Ryan and Ross, to Grant Street to watch Nairn lift the same cup in a final against Forres Mechanics. It was a wonderful experience taking the boys to the game and joining in the vociferous support that travelled to Inverness that day from Nairn.

However, I would acknowledge that the loss of such great sides as Ross County, Caley, Inverness Thistle and Elgin to the Scottish League has greatly diminished the prestige of this competition. Ross County and Caley Thistle still enter the North Cup, with rules governing the playing personnel they field because they are now in the higher echelons of the Scottish game. But fans of my vintage who can recall those great sides and great matches of the 1960s know we will never see those days again. I mentioned earlier the 1966 final and replay: there were upwards of 3,000 at each game. I suspect that at the final in 2006 with Forres the attendance would barely have touched 800.

My other son, Sean, Ryan's twin, I must add is not a sports enthusiast. Artistic yes – energetic no. He has, however, developed a wicked sense of humour which endears him to many. When the twins were about nine I took them Station Park for their first taste of football. Ryan was hooked from the start. As for Sean? Well I detected from the outset complete indifference to this 'exciting' day out dad had planned for them both. When we got to the ground I felt we should head to the barriers at the side of the pitch looking across to the cowshed from the eighteen-yard-line so we could get a good view. It brought back happy memories of when my dad took me to games as a legitimate paying customer through the turnstiles. My suspicions that Sean was indifferent to the sport his dad had a passion for were confirmed when he leaned on the barrier, waggled a finger towards the goalposts at either end of the pitch and enquired: 'Dad what are they?' It was his way of telling me 'get me out of here'. He was taken home at half-time and has never darkened the turnstiles of Station Park since.

A social evening followed Nairn's 1966 win over Caley in the Royal Hotel, but a week later a dinner and dance was held to properly mark the occasion of three North Cup wins in four years.

A hat-trick against Rothes on 23 April brought Johnston's tally for the season to 51, and at the end of 1965-66 Nairn finished in sixth place with 35 points from 30 games. Johnston, by then, had added ten more strikes, bringing his total to 61 to regain the title of the league's top scorer. Andy Kerr of Caley was second on 41 and Billy Smith's contribution to the Nairn cause could be measured by his haul of 32 goals.

There wasn't much signing activity during the summer of 1966 but Nairn did secure the services of winger Jocky Clark. Eric Geddes, meanwhile, continued to keep abreast of developments in the game by attending another SFA coaching course at Largs.

Tommy Gemmell, the Celtic and Scotland full-back trained one after-noon pre-season with Nairn. He was staying in Inverness and was catching up with acquaintances, John Mackintosh from Union Street in Nairn and Willie Fraser who owned the Lion Hotel in Auldearn. Gemmell and Johnston were later to lock horns in opposition when Celtic played Aberdeen in the 1967 Scottish Cup final at Hampden Park.

A review of the next, 1966-67, season provides evidence that Eric Geddes, despite the loss of so many key players, who were no doubt enticed by better money on offer from the bigger clubs, had again assembled a side that was capable of challenging for honours. He introduced a 4-2-4 system for the opening game of the season against Clach, which didn't go down entirely well with the fans after a 1-1 draw. A 3-3 draw with Elgin in the Highland League Cup followed, and Johnston was back in the groove with two goals, to be followed with a hat-trick the following week in a 5-4 win against Buckie. A Keith Rattray double at Elgin knocked Nairn out of the Highland League Cup but Nairn's league form was solid.

Rumours surfaced in October 1966 that Johnston of Nairn and Grant of Elgin were seeking a change of clubs. On 5 November Nairn beat Lossie 2-1 at Grant Park with Johnston scoring one of the goals. It was to be his last before his departure to Aberdeen. With Nairn on seventeen points from eleven league games, they were again title contenders.

Off to Pittodrie

Many people can remember where they were the moment they heard President John F Kennedy was assassinated or that Elvis Presley had died. I remember clearly the day I heard the news that Davy had been transferred to Aberdeen. I met Charlie McGowan, a neighbour who lived round the corner in John Street, when he broke the news to me on the evening of 7 November 1966.

Charlie was one of the gang who would join us at Station Park on training nights. He had a tremendous burst of speed I recall in his younger days and was quite a good keeper, so was often selected to go in goal for the practice matches with the County players.

The news came right out of the blue. Even the *Press & Journal*, the Aberdeen daily which was usually up to speed with events at Pittodrie before they had happened, was taken by surprise. But credit to *P&J* sports journalist Bill McAllister whose finger was always on the pulse with events behind the scenes in the Highland League. He reported on 3

October that Johnston wanted a move from Nairn. And later coverage of the transfer confirmed that Aberdeen had in fact made their move six weeks before the deal was sealed.

I was heartbroken by Davy's departure and so were hundreds of Nairn fans. The County committee at the time came in for stick from some quarters for selling their best asset and a player who was hero worshipped by the supporters. Some never forgave them. But the reality was they could not stand in Davy's way.

Some fans said Davy had been coerced into moving to Aberdeen and was reluctant to leave Nairn. But it was Davy's personal choice and Sandy Finlayson, a committee member of Nairn County at that time had this to say on the issue:

'Davy wanted to make the move to Pittodrie. He knew it was his last chance to become a full-time pro. By now he was married and had a young family to support and he wanted to give it a go [a view confirmed by Davy himself in an interview with Bill McAllister which we will come to later]. Tom Walls, the Nairn County chairman, did all the negotiating at the time and Eddie Turnbull came to Nairn to speak to Davy and persuaded him to join Aberdeen.'

Sandy Finlayson, however, recalls that the Nairn County side of that era was not a one-man show: 'We had many fantastic players and it was often said that we had the best team never to have won the Highland League although we came very close a couple of times. Our centre-half Tommy Sanderson and goalkeeper Kenny Mackenzie could have graced many a Scottish League side. We had Alex Bowman who was a wizard on the wing and Alex Young who was an accomplished full-back. Then of course there was Davy's best mate Chic. He was as strong as an ox and a gifted player too. Together their partnership flourished on Davy's return from Tynecastle and of course they were to team up again later at Caley.'

The *Nairnshire Telegraph* revealed that negotiations had been ongoing for about a week before the transfer was agreed. The Nairn committee met on Sunday, 6 November and decided they would not stand in way of the player's advancement. Turnbull visited Nairn himself to get Johnston to put to pen to paper the following day. Davy was three weeks short of his 24th birthday.

Even at that late stage there is an indication of self-doubt when Johnston told the local newspaper he felt it was time for a change 'and that Mr Turnbull had been able to iron out my doubts about stepping up'. In the twenty months since Turnbull breezed into Pittodrie like a full-scale hurricane, the change in the club's fortunes was dramatic. From an under-performing club struggling in the First Division, they were now sitting third in the league behind Rangers in what was to prove a fruitless pursuit of all-conquering Celtic in the race for the league flag.

In October of that year Turnbull himself was named as the top student at an SFA coaching course at Largs, and Martin Buchan and Ian Taylor, two teenagers from the Banks o' Dee 'A' team, were recruited as he continued on his root and branch review of his playing pool.

Turnbull's credentials as a top coach in fact were widely acknowledged and he was in big demand. Some months after his move to Aberdeen he was apparently offered the Scotland job in succession to Jock Stein but turned that down. And just a week before he signed Johnston, Turnbull rejected an offer to move to Rangers, although he admitted having held talks with the Ibrox directors. Whether Turnbull was head-hunted as assistant to manager Scot Symon or to succeed him is not entirely clear. There may even have been two approaches a year or more apart. In his autobiography, Turnbull describes the sticking point as being his total control of team affairs, something the Rangers directors were not prepared to concede. Turnbull remained at Pittodrie.

Interviewed by Bill McAllister, Davy spoke about his change of heart to return to the Scottish League after a five-year absence. Therein lies further underlying evidence of the insecurities which bedevilled his career. He talked about a previous approach from the Dons during Pearson's management which he had spurned because he feared their expectations of him might be too great and the Dons were looking for some kind of 'wonderman':

'I feel the time has come for a change of club. Aberdeen are the only Scottish club I would consider joining,' he told the *P&J* journalist.

'The first indication came six weeks ago but there were no developments and it seemed he would stay at Station Park,' McAllister wrote. But a call from Turnbull to Tom Walls triggered off a chain of events which took Johnston to Pittodrie at last: 'I did not commit myself right away,' said Johnston. 'I went home to talk it over with my wife. Then I told Mr Walls I'd like to see what Mr Turnbull had to offer.'

And turning to the news of Rangers' bid to secure Turnbull's services the previous week, Johnston had this to say: 'If Mr Turnbull had taken the Rangers job last week I might never have signed. He's a very persuasive man. I considered it a very lucky break. One of the main reasons why Mr Turnbull succeeded where others failed was that he was able to iron out my doubts. The last time I refused the Dons I was getting plenty of goals in the Highland League and would have been expected to do likewise for them. I felt that, like all the other clubs, they wanted a 'wonderman' and if I didn't get goals right away I would be out in the cold. But

Mr Turnbull made the position clear that he is not looking for miracles from me. I'll be given time to settle and a full chance to prove myself. He had seen me in action for the North Select against Dunfermline at Inverness last season. In addition, the terms are such that they mean security for me and my family. We are looking forward to living in Aberdeen.'

In the world of football, signing a player of the calibre of Johnston can often just be down to a stroke of luck and perhaps someone being in the right place at the right time. Such was the case in Davy's move to Aberdeen. That he was happy enough working in the laundry and play-ing part-time football for his home-town team there is no doubt. But when I spoke to Eddie Turnbull about Davy's transfer from Nairn and how it devastated me and every County fan at the time, his response was immediate: 'Well you can blame your local bobby for that!'

Turnbull recalled that Aberdeen FC had been tipped off by local police sergeant Jimmy Thomson of the Moray & Nairn Constabulary. And it was he who proved to be the conduit through which Davy and his young family packed their bags and moved to what everyone hoped would be a bright new future for them in the Granite City. Thomson was a close friend of Davy's wife Margaret's family, who lived in Auldearn. He was a regular at Station Park, both on duty and off. He did much of the spadework behind the scenes and helped persuade Davy that it was an opportunity not to be missed for him and his family.

Margaret said she, too, had to convince Davy that it was a chance he could not afford to pass up when Aberdeen came calling. 'The house we were living in was rented from the education authority on the Inverness Road beside what was then Nairn Academy but is now Rosebank Primary School,' recalled Margaret. 'It was in a shocking state but we couldn't afford to be choosy and it was home. Sharon was two and young David was a month old when we moved to Aberdeen. I had to persuade Davy to take up Aberdeen's offer but Jimmy came round to speak to him as well. I don't think he thought he was good enough. Despite what every-one said about his ability, Davy always had his doubts and definitely lacked confidence. He was worried he wouldn't cope with the step up to the First Division and would happily have played for Nairn and worked at the laundry for the rest of his days.'

Margaret, however, said her husband realised it was a chance for them to get on their feet financially: 'He agreed to go but he always promised that he would be back in Nairn for Sharon to start school. That was always his plan.' It was a plan he stuck to, which meant in 1969 he broke his contract with Aberdeen to move back north.

Margaret recalls they had a flat at 11 Cairnfield Place, Rosemount Aberdeen. 'It had two bedrooms and we were on the ground floor and Jens Petersen lived above. Jimmy Wilson had been in the flat before us and club skipper Harry Melrose was in the next block of flats. The idea that Davy could have commuted from Nairn was never even considered. It would not have been practical. We had £2 10s (£2.50) deducted for rent by the club each week.'

Jimmy the Fixer

As for Jimmy The Fixer, I suppose that today, in the way football business is conducted, he could claim a sizeable cut as an agent for arranging the transfer of a player of Davy Johnston's calibre. But Jimmy Thomson was simply looking after the interests of a young family, hoping he could help them find a better life.

In my childhood I never had any direct dealings with Sgt Thomson. But I know from what my parents told me how highly respected he was in the local community. I don't know if he ever really did give a lad a clip on the lug or a kick up the backside for erring on the wrong side of the law – but you'll catch my drift if I tell you he had gained a reputation for being that type of bobby. A bit of common-sense prevailed and a quiet word with an offending youngster's parents would be his style rather than dragging them 'under the town clock' where the Burgh police court sat once every month.

At the time of writing, Jimmy was elderly and frail, living in retirement in the Haughs of Cromdale. Sadly, before the publication of this book he died. Fittingly, at his funeral service there was a retiring collection for some of his favourite charities.

Jimmy's son-in-law Sandy McMorran, himself a retired police superintendent from the Grampian Force who retired to his native Nairn, explained that his father-in-law was a cousin of Irene Scott, the wife of Aberdeen trainer, Teddy. Sandy told me his father-in-law was very frail but he kindly spoke to him before his death on my behalf about the circumstances surrounding Davy's transfer.

Sandy reported back that Jimmy confirmed his role. Jimmy had tipped off Teddy Scott that the time might be right to make an approach to Johnston, whose scoring exploits were adorning the pages of the *Press & Journal*, the *Sunday Mail* and *Sunday Post* and several national dailies which in those days gave north football far greater recognition than it receives today.

Jimmy Thomson was a footballer himself, having played full-back for Fraserburgh. But he had given it up to pursue his police career: 'Jimmy told me he got in touch with Teddy because Davy was just scoring goals for fun in those days,' said Sandy:

'Teddy came up with Irene and stayed at the caravan site at the east beach in Nairn and took in a couple of matches. He was obviously impressed because, the next thing, Jimmy got a phone call from Teddy to say Aberdeen wanted to sign Davy. Jimmy remembered clearly that Davy signed for Aberdeen in front of himself, Margaret, Eddie Turnbull and Teddy on the kitchen table of his police house at the corner of Albert Street, across from Tom Walls' surgery. Jimmy said at the table there was no question about having to persuade Davy to put pen to paper. Davy was really quite nonchalant about it all, as if it was no big deal.

'I assume terms had already been agreed between the clubs because my father-in-law's recollection is there was no one present from County when he signed,' and this was confirmed by Margaret herself.

Sandy's dad, James McMorran, was my music teacher at Millbank School. Totally blind, his other senses compensated for the loss of his sight: 'I was a regular myself at Station Park,' recalled Sandy, 'and dad could tell me the score when I got home just by hearing the roars from the crowd as he sat in the garden of our home in Manse Road. He always asked how many Johnston scored today?'

Sandy, who married Jimmy Thomson's daughter Kathleen, said his favourite Nairn team of the 1960s was: Mackenzie, Cadenhead, Young, Cameron, Sanderson, Allan, Leighton, Shields, Johnston, Clyne and Bowman.

'It was an incredible side and for me and other youngsters the sun could rise and set on Davy Johnston. He was an incredible talent and the headmaster at the school where dad taught, James Stark, always said that lad would play for Scotland some day. Alex Bowman, I remember, had a metal plate in his head and he was never allowed to head the ball. Jackie Shields was a tough Dundonian and he was a great dribbler with fantastic close control. Then of course there was Rodwill Clyne who like Davy had a very powerful shot. He was coming towards the end of his career by the time he arrived at Nairn. But Rod loved life and lived it to the full. Looking after himself was never high on Rod's agenda and he would often get a telling off from Eric Geddes because he would not think twice about running out onto the pitch puffing at a cigarette.'

Although he watched Davy both at Station Park and during his years at Pittodrie, Sandy McMorran never met the man personally until their paths crossed years later on a drainage scheme down by the coast at

Portsoy: 'I had been called out to investigate an alleged suspicious death after bones were found on a drainage project down by Portsoy beach. I was a Detective Chief Inspector in Aberdeen and the first reports suggested we could have a potential murder scene to deal with. It turned out it to be an ancient burial ground and there was nothing sinister at all. But the man at the controls of the digger was Davy Johnston who was working as a labourer with a firm of contractors.

'We had a long chat about his footballing days. It was the first and only time I ever spoke to the man and he was a totally unassuming and modest individual. I was surprised when he knew me because I was of the same age as his cousin, the late Jackie Urquhart, who was one of his biggest fans.'

The *Press & Journal* reported that Aberdeen had paid a 'substantial fee' for the Nairn sharpshooter and that the Dons had succeeded where many other clubs had failed. St Johnstone, Dundee, Dundee United, Falkirk and Aberdeen were just some of the Scottish clubs who had been queuing up to lure Davy away from the Highland League over the previous five years but he had refused all offers. Dundee were reported to have made an offer of £8,000 for Johnston the previous year. But there is no doubt that the Edinburgh connection between Eddie Turnbull and Hearts manager Tommy Walker was a major factor in his move to Pittodrie. Eddie knew Tommy well during his days with Hibs. It was only when Turnbull made a direct approach that Hearts lifted a clause in the contract of Davy's release so he could rejoin Nairn but could not sign for another Scottish League club.

Davy's departure to Pittodrie in 1966 was to mark the beginning of a nine-year-exile from Station Park. When the player quit Aberdeen in 1969, Turnbull would be left frustrated because he believed Davy had never fulfilled his potential.

A Scoring Debut:
'The brains behind the forward line'

Turnbull told me that when Davy Johnston arrived at Pittodrie he put him under the wing of skipper Harry Melrose, who had been outside-left in Jock Stein's Dunfermline team which won the Scottish Cup in 1961. Turnbull was aware Davy was a sensitive lad, but he wanted to find out what made him tick. The manager knew also he had a rare talent which still had to reach its full potential. His aim was to transform the player into the international footballer everybody believed he was capable of becoming.

Turnbull had promised Johnston that he would ease him in gradually. But it was clear that Aberdeen fans watching him play for the reserves awaited his first-team debut with eager anticipation. Pittodrie regularly attracted attendances of over 30,000 for Old Firm matches in those days and sometimes crowds of 4,000 would attend reserve games.

Davy's first outing was against St Mirren 'A' on 11 November 1966 and the *P&J* would report that he had an impressive debut, scoring one and laying on two goals in a crushing 7-2 victory. Johnston was 'the brains behind the home forward line', said the *P&J*: 'he contributed to his team's success as much off the ball as on it.'

'I really enjoyed the game,' said Davy. 'I found the pace a bit faster than the Highland League but I'm confident with full-time training I'll be alright.'

By the end of November there were calls for his promotion to the first team. Francis Munro's transfer from Dundee United had triggered an eight-game winning run for the first team, but the wheels fell off the cart when Aberdeen went down 0-1 to Falkirk at Brockville on 10 December. Meanwhile, back at Pittodrie, Johnston, now turned 24, was playing another starring role for the reserves in a 5-0 win over the Bairns' reserves. Davy, in fact, had just completed his first full week's training at Pittodrie because it took several weeks to get his family settled into their club flat in Aberdeen.

Anxious not to lose further ground to Celtic in the title race, Turnbull named Johnston, who had scored in every reserve game he played, in his starting line-up for the following week's encounter with Stirling Albion at Annfield on 17 December. Far from giving him time to acclimatise, as he had promised, Turnbull pitched Davy into the first team a month after signing him.

In the first months of 1966-67 Turnbull had continued to tinker with his team. This was far from a settled side. Johnston in fact was Aberdeen's fifth new introduction in recent weeks. Future Manchester United and Scotland captain Martin Buchan made his bow on 8 October. Full-back Jim Hermiston debuted alongside Munro on 15 October, and a week later speedy young forward Ian Taylor wrested the No 9 shirt from Ernie Winchester.

Taylor spearheaded the line-up for eight matches prior to Johnston's introduction to the centre-forward position, and Taylor would remain at Pittodrie as a squad player until 1974. The man who ultimately stood aside for Johnston, however, was Winchester, who had played in thirteen of Aberdeen's fourteen league games before Davy's arrival, but rarely got a look in thereafter. At the end of the season Winchester went off to play in the United States for a couple of years before resurfacing at Hearts.

This is not to say that Ernie Winchester and Davy Johnston were similar kinds of player. Far from it. David Innes describes Winchester as a 'bustling striker, a hardman who would not last 45 minutes these days before he was red-carded. His relationship with the fans was love-hate, depending on whether he had just scored with a brave diving header or missed an open goal from two yards out. He was Aberdeen's main centre-forward in an era of austerity, but it is a matter of debate whether he deserves the legendary status he is accorded on afcheritage.org website.'

Nevertheless, Winchester was a goalscoring machine, 91 goals in all competitions from just 169 appearances. Turnbull must have had high hopes that Davy Johnston could match that supply of goals while bringing other attributes to Aberdeen's play. Turnbull was shrewd, too, in handing Davy his debut not at Pittodrie, Ibrox or Parkhead, but at tiny Stirling Albion, near the foot of the league, whose gates barely exceeded 1,000, and which must have seemed a home from home for a new recruit from the Highland League.

Following that defeat at Falkirk, it was important for Aberdeen to get back on the rails because on Christmas Eve they were to play Celtic in what was already being dubbed a title 'decider' at Pittodrie. I didn't know it at the time, but my father was already making plans to take myself and my brother Sandford to that match.

Johnston couldn't have asked for a better debut. He maintained his goal-a-game record by scoring (to put Aberdeen 4-1 up) in an emphatic 6-2 win at Stirling. Norman Macdonald, the *P&J* sportswriter wrote: 'I have a hunch that manager Turnbull produced his trump card on the eve of the league "decider" against Celtic by introducing Dave Johnston at centre-forward and switching Ian Taylor to the left wing. The former Highland League player made a stylish debut and kept up his record of having scored in every game since his arrival at Pittodrie.'

The scene was set for a mighty showdown with the Parkhead side in Aberdeen the following week. Celtic were five points ahead of Rangers and six ahead of the Dons, so to describe the game as a 'decider' was an exaggeration. It must be remembered, however, that in those days it was only two points for a win. Nevertheless the media hype certainly helped capture the public's imagination and 30,000 fans, myself included, were there to witness the confrontation between two of the title contenders.

Celtic's last defeat in the league was back in February against Stirling Albion, of all teams. And let's not forget either that they were already through to the last eight of the European Cup. Would Aberdeen be the team to burst the Parkhead bubble? Turnbull began the mind games by proclaiming early in the week: 'We fear no one at Pittodrie and we'll let Celtic do the worrying.' The stage was set for a classic encounter and the teams didn't disappoint.

At eleven years of age, this was my first big match and it was only when I came to research this book that I realised it was only Davy's second appearance for the Aberdeen first team. The importance of the game in the context of the league championship I don't think had really registered with me. But I went there in the full expectation that I would see Davy scoring goals.

I have a vague recollection that my fare on the bus, which was organised by the Seaforth Club in Nairn, cost 2 shillings and 6 pence – that's 12½ pence in today's money.

When my brother and I boarded the bus with my father I was shocked to find another schoolboy, Raymond Grant, wearing a Celtic shirt. To my young mind I thought everyone in Nairn would have started supporting Aberdeen after Davy's transfer. But by then many of my classmates were dyed-in-the-wool Old Firm fans and they weren't for changing.

I can't describe the excitement I felt when I heard we were going to the game. But being Christmas Eve added to the sense of occasion. I had never been to a major city before and everything seemed so big to me. One thing which stuck in my mind was the Christmas lights and the size of the street lamps, which had a big hook at the top where the light was fitted, providing illumination across what seemed the vast expanse of North Anderson Drive. This was an area of the city I was to become familiar with in later years when my wife trained as a midwife at the Aberdeen Royal Infirmary and I had a short spell working on the news-desk at the *Press & Journal*'s HQ at the Lang Stracht.

I had never seen high-rise flats before and at that tender age it's certainly not a place I would have liked to live by choice. In my later years, of course, I was to visit the Granite City often when my wife was a nurse there and I can understand why Aberdonians have pride in their home town.

On the morning of the big match the *Press & Journal* ran a feature one would normally expect for a Cup final with pen pics of all the players expected to play. Come the event, Aberdeen's line-up was: Clark, Whyte, Shewan, Munro, McMillan, Petersen, Wilson, Melrose, Johnston, Smith, Taylor. Celtic's eleven was: Simpson, Gemmell, O'Neil, Murdoch, McNeill, Clark, Chalmers, Auld, McBride, Wallace, Lennox. Of course, nine of those Celtic stars a few months later would belong to the first

British side to win the European Cup. Jim Craig and Jimmy Johnstone would play in Lisbon, O'Neil and McBride missing out.

My father, in fact, had no experience of going to such a big match and like the rest of the 28,000 crowd I am sure we paid at the turnstiles. Having no experience of being at Pittodrie before, we somehow landed at the Merkland stand, known as the King Street end at that time, in among the Celtic support. No seating of course in those days and I had never witnessed such a mass of humanity in such a confined space. For safety reasons my father wisely took us down to the front against the boundary wall behind the goal.

I was in awe of the noise that the Celtic fans behind me were making and the match certainly lived up to all its promise. My hero Davy, with 28,000 pairs of eyes upon this red-kitted newcomer, never got among the goals. According to the *P&J* he was shackled by Billy McNeill, but Melrose and Jimmy Wilson posed problems for Celtic down the right flank. My recollection that Lennox scored for Celtic and Melrose for the Dons in a thrill-packed 1-1 draw proved correct. The veteran Celtic keeper Ronnie Simpson was hailed a hero by the Celtic legions when he made an incredible save six minutes from time, when Francis Munro cracked in what looked like a 'homer' from ten yards. But the agile Simpson arched his back and got his finger tips to the ball and turned it over the bar.

'It would have been a tragedy if either side had lost,' the *P& J* sportingly acknowledged. One cannot help but wonder how Davy felt after 90 minutes' combat with Billy McNeill, one of the giants of Scottish football, or what McNeill thought of the nimble upstart pitted against him. So much for the gentle introduction that Turnbull had promised Davy.

For me, however, the drama didn't end at the final whistle. Rather than wait for the crowds to disperse, my father took my brother and I by the hand and led us up the terracing and down the steps out of the enclosure towards Pittodrie Street. I was becoming increasingly alarmed because I was getting caught up in the vast crowd and couldn't keep my feet on the ground. I lost my grip on my father's hand and, terrified, I tumbled to the floor. There was nothing he nor Sandford could do as they got swept away into the distance by the crowd. I had lost one of my shoes and for a few moments I struggled on the ground in sheer terror before a man picked me up and literally threw me behind a burger van where I found sanctuary in the natural funnel that was created as the milling masses swarmed round the vehicle.

It might be an exaggeration to say that chap saved my life but it certainly felt like it at the time. As soon as the crowds began to subside my dad, who was frantic by this time, returned to find me safely beside the van. Within minutes we had retrieved my shoe, trampled but nevertheless still serviceable. So what a tale we had to tell my brothers and sister on our return to Nairn that Christmas Eve evening.

Aberdeen came under fire for not having enough police on duty at the game and while I offer no view on that subject I still have a vivid recollection of my experience that day. I know I was very lucky. Four years later, 66 fans lost their lives on stairway 13 at Ibrox when railings gave way and hundreds of fans piled down the stairs on top of each other. Many of the victims were children.

Cup Final against Lisbon Lions

After the draw with Celtic, Aberdeen enjoyed a 4-0 win over Kilmarnock and a 5-2 victory over Dundee. Following the game against the Dens Park side, the *P&J* reported that Johnston 'confirmed the impression that the Dons have at last found a forward with the powers of leadership. The former Highland League sharpshooter was most unlucky not to get his name on the scoresheet.'

Those wins took the Dons into second place, but only one point was taken from away fixtures at St Johnstone and Clyde. A midweek fixture with Rangers now loomed at Pittodrie and a 'football special' train was laid on for fans from Inverness railway station.

Turnbull changed his formation, switching Davy from centre-forward – after six games in the middle – to the left wing. Ernie Winchester was briefly restored to the No 9 shirt, presumably because he would better withstand the battering meted out by Rangers' stopper Ron McKinnon.

Johnston scored his first goal against the Old Firm to the delight of fans from the north that night, and a brilliant one it was. But a double strike from transfer-listed Rangers striker George McLean secured a 2-1 victory for the Gers. Aberdeen then lost 1-2 at home to Dunfermline, with Davy again on the wing, leaving their championship hopes virtually extinguished.

But the Scottish Cup provided a big incentive and Johnston was to figure prominently in Aberdeen's surge to the final at Hampden Park in late April, against a team that was to be crowned champions of Europe in Lisbon the following month. Back at No 9, Davy scored two goals against Dundee in the first round and two more against St Johnstone in the second. Both opponents were soundly beaten 5-0. The cup-tie with St Johnstone was Bobby Brown's last as manager of the Perth club before taking over the reins of Scotland.

Davy's first competitive hat-trick for the Dons came against Airdrie in the league on 11 February, bringing his tally to eight since breaking into the first team in mid-December.

There was a fanfare of publicity in February when Aberdeen bought Leeds striker Jim Storrie. Initial claims that the fee was a record £20,000 were later played down and the figure of £12,500 became the consensus. The former Airdrie player had scored 67 goals in 156 appearances for the Elland Road side. But his stay at Pittodrie was to be a brief one.

The quarter-final draw presented a tougher proposition with an away tie at Hibs. In a league dress rehearsal on 25 February, Hibs edged home 1-0 at Easter Road. But Turnbull sought to reassure the Aberdeen faithful, saying Hibs had their strongest team out and Aberdeen could still improve. Johnston raised his scoring tally to eleven goals in an eight-game sequence with a double in a league match against John Harvey's Hearts, which the Dons won 3-0. Hearts, of course, had been Davy's first senior club and it was exactly this scenario former manager Tommy Walker feared when he let the player return to Nairn six years earlier.

The much-anticipated cup quarter-final against Hibs saw Aberdeen trailing 0-1, but Johnston was instrumental in keeping the Dons alive in the cup, supplying a perfectly placed free-kick for Jimmy Smith to bag the late equaliser.

The replay eleven days later, on Wednesday, 22 March, drew a record midweek Pittodrie crowd of 44,000, with gate receipts of £8,127. Hibs were almost dead and buried after Aberdeen surged into a two-goal lead in fifteen minutes. The final scoreline was 3-0, with two goals from the recalled Winchester and one from Jim Storrie, but the entire Aberdeen forward line was praised for the way they tore through Hibs' defence.

Aberdeen's league form fell away. They were to finish fourth behind Clyde and way behind the Old Firm. But they had a cup semi-final with Dundee United to look forward to, and that match was a sell-out at neutral Dens Park. The game turned into a bit of a damp squib, with solid defending seeing Aberdeen across the finishing line courtesy of a fourth-minute own-goal by Tommy Millar, who was consoled by his team-mates and opponents alike at the final whistle.

With the Cup final beckoning, Jock Macdonald, the Inverness Thistle chairman – who had a stand named in his honour at the Caledonian Thistle stadium – announced his club would run a train with seven coaches to Hampden on 29 April. Few people owned private cars in those days and the journey down the A9 to Glasgow took over five hours.

Meanwhile, Jock Stein's Celtic had already accounted for Dukla Prague 3-1 in the first leg of the European Cup semi-final. Aberdeen were under no illusions about the task they faced. Scotland beat World Cup winners England 3-2 in a memorable international at Wembley on 15 April and four days later Celtic and Aberdeen played a 0-0 league draw at Parkhead in a rehearsal for the Cup final. Turnbull was missing from the Aberdeen bench that night and the *P&J* reported he was confined to bed with a stomach complaint. Celtic held Dukla to a goalless draw in Prague in midweek so they would go into the final on the Saturday having secured their place in the final against Inter-Milan in Lisbon.

Determined to bring the Scottish Cup back to Aberdeen for the first time since 1946-47, Turnbull – whose autobiography confirmed he had contracted hepatitis ten days previously – rose from his sick bed to prepare his players. He accompanied them on the team bus to their hotel at Gleneagles on the Friday afternoon. But at noon on matchday the players were told the unwelcome news that their manager was not fit to travel to Hampden with them. To add to their woes, the team bus got caught up in traffic as thousands of fans headed down to the match from the north-east.

Goalkeeper Bobby Clark was a part-timer and in the final year of his PE degree at Jordanhill College. He had had an exam brought forward so he could play in the quarter-final replay against Hibs and on the day of the final he made his own way to Hampden, expecting to find his teammates already in the dressing room when he arrived at 1.45pm:

'After about 30 minutes there was still no sign of the team,' recalled Bobby. 'I popped my head down the tunnel just to check that I had come on the right day. The pipe band was playing and crowds were filing in, so I knew I was in the right place. I think it must have been around 2.30 when the bus, minus Eddie Turnbull, finally arrived and, as you could imagine, it was a rush to get changed and onto the field. It was sad that preparation was so hurried, as I felt this affected the team. We never really played until the final twenty minutes. Not having Eddie, who was ill and had to be left at the hotel, was a big disappointment. Davie Shaw did a good job mustering the team but Eddie was the boss and he was missed. It really was a great team, though, and Davy brought great speed and could hit a ball with either foot. As a goalie I can attest to his ability to hit the ball. At practice I doubt if anyone hit the ball harder or truer than Davy.'

Celtic triumphed 2-0 with goals from Wallace in 42 and 49 minutes. I was attending an Air Training Corps jumble sale in the drill hall in Nairn and kept in touch with events at Hampden through a small solid-state transistor radio. I was crushed by the result as, no doubt, were the Aberdeen fans in the 126,102 crowd at the national stadium.

And what of Davy in the Scottish Cup final? The evidence is thin, but perhaps Billy McNeill had pocketed the raw newcomer in that Christmas league clash at Pittodrie. Turnbull responded by playing Jim Storrie at No 9, both at Hampden and in the league game at Parkhead ten days earlier. Davy played outside-left, facing the Bhoys' right-back Jim Craig who, desperate to keep his place against Inter-Milan, needed to impress manager Jock Stein. He appears to have done so, for Craig notes in his autobiography – *A Lion Looks Back* – 'I knew myself that I had played well [at Hampden] and the press coverage on the following days tended to agree with that. I even got a rare "well done" from Jock Stein.' If player, manager, and press concurred that Craig had played well, the obvious conclusion is that the winger against him, Davy Johnston, had not.

The question on everyone's lips, however, was would Aberdeen have won the cup had Eddie Turnbull been there to guide them that day? Sportswriter Norman Macdonald conceded probably not. But he was convinced Turnbull would have made tactical changes as the game developed. Aberdeen, said Macdonald, were too defensively minded. There was no lack of honest effort but the sparkle and sense of urgency evident in previous rounds was missing. Turnbull, he added, had succeeded in building a well-organised defensive system but still lacked the magic touch in attack.

In May, Johnston scored four goals in a 7-0 friendly win for the Dons against Arbroath to mark the opening of Lads Club's new pavilion at Woodside in Aberdeen. The match was an ideal warm-up before the team embarked on the biggest adventure of their lives – a seven-week tour of Canada and the USA. Turnbull's health was, however, still giving cause for concern and it was unclear whether he would be able to travel with his players.

In less than six months Johnston had become a Pittodrie personality. He had played in 26 consecutive first-team games (twenty in the league and six in the Scottish Cup) commencing with his debut on 17 December 1966, ending with the Cup final on 29 April 1967, scoring fourteen goals (ten in the league and four in the Cup) – an excellent scoring rate by any standards. With hindsight, the statistics show it would never get better for Davy Johnston.

I managed to secure video footage of both the Scottish Cup final and the memorable President's Cup final with Wolves in Los Angeles, which was the highlight of the 1967 summer tour. My son Ryan watched the footage with me in awe, not just at Johnston but the whole Aberdeen team and the quality of play he was witnessing. What has happened to our national game? I fear we will never see the likes again when a

Young Davy studying at his schoolwork

Some of Nairn County's cup double-winning squad of 1963-64: Back row (L-R) Eric Geddes (trainer), Stuart Robertson, Rodwill Clyne, Andy Cadenhead, Kenny Mackenzie, Jim Cameron, Tom Walls (chairman), Alex Young, Bob Gordon (committee), Ally Chisholm ,John Bochel (kitman); Front: Ian MacLennan, Sandy Matheson, Davy Johnston, Chic Allan, Ronnie Mair, Alex Bowman, Tommy Sanderson

A lads night out in the Supper Room at a dance at the Public Hall in Nairn. (left to right) Alan Watson, Davy, Billy Gibson, George Macleod

Nairn fans waving their banner in jubilation after winning the North of Scotland Cup replay 3-2 against Caley on 26 March 1966 at the home of Clachnaccudin, Grant Street, Inverness. The first game, played before 3,000 fans, ended in a 4-4 draw

Captain Andy Cadenhead (with trainer Eric Geddes to his left) holds the cup aloft with players (left to right) Davy Johnston, Billy Smith, Alex Cameron, Alex Young, 16-year-old David Ross, Johnnie Nairn, Ronnie Murray and the jubilant Nairn supporters

Another team and crowd scene. Davy Johnston is the second Nairn player from the left

Triumphant Davy with the North of Scotland Cup and committee members James 'Turk' Fraser and John Edwards proudly carrying the base of the trophy across the Clach pitch

Up for the Cup! Aberdeen players pose in April 1967 outside Pittodrie before leaving for their hotel in Gleneagles. Johnston is squatting, second from the right. The Dons lost the Scottish Cup final 0-2 to Celtic. Manager Eddie Turnbull was unwell and unable to attend the game. The team bus also arrived late at Hampden Park

Davy established himself as Pittodrie's prince of penalty-takers. He is seen here firing the ball high past Dundee United's Sandy Davie for the Dons' fifth goal on 14 October 1967. It was Davy's second goal in a 6-0 win

Posed picture of Davy Johnston at Pittodrie, with empty terracing in the background

Sunning themselves at the poolside at the Hilton Hotel in Washington in 1967 during
the Dons' tour of Canada and the USA – Davy, centre, and Ally Shewan (right).
Only things missing are the knotted hankies

Hearts keeper Garland and Aberdeen's Robb go down, but Davy Johnston (centre)
keeps his feet and nets Aberdeen's second goal in a 2-0 win on 10 February 1968

Davy Johnston has a go himself, but Clyde centre-half Jim Fraser steps in to hook the ball clear on 24 August 1968. Aberdeen lost this League Cup-tie 0-2

Johnston scores the Dons' second goal against Airdrie at Pittodrie on 5 April 1969. Aberdeen won 3-1, but this would be Davy's last ever goal for the Dons

A month after scoring his last goal, at home to Airdrie, Johnston packs up and leaves his club flat after walking out on Aberdeen. It brought an end to his senior football career in May 1969

Caledonian FC 1969-70 Back (L-R) Malcolm Cowie, Bobby Noble, Dave Bennett, Andy Beattie, Alan Presslie, Graham MacInnes, Les Cowie.
Front (L-R) Billy Little, Chic Allan, Davy Johnston, Sandy Finnie, Freddie Neild

Caley, Highland League Cup winners 1969-70. Chic Allan scored twice in a 2-1 win over Peterhead. Back (L-R) Freddie Neild, Davy Johnston, Bryan Munro, Bobby Noble, Andy Beattie, Graham McInnes, Sandy Finnie. Front (L-R) Billy Little, Malcolm Cowie, Chic Allan, Jim McPherson (president), Alan Presslie, Dave Bennett, Neil Smith (secretary)

Caley, 1969-70 winners Highland League Cup and Scottish Qualifying (North) Cup. Back: Stapleton, Middleton, Finnie, Noble, MacDonald, MacKenzie, Sutherland, Cowie, Bennett, Fyfe, Patience (trainer). Front: Cowie (coach), Allan, Smith (secretary), Johnston, McPherson (president), Presslie, Veighey (treasurer), McInnes, Lowrie (vice-president)

Caley, champions 1970-71.
Back (L-R) Munro, Neild, Park, Forsyth, Allan, Slater, McGregor, Mackintosh.
Centre (L-R) Lowrie, Lynas, Lockhart, Anderson, Noble, Mackenzie, Bennett.
Front (L-R) Smith (secretary), Presslie, McPherson (president), Johnston, Veighey (treasurer)

Caley players get a boardroom briefing as the team prepare for their Scottish Cup-tie
with Thistle, 13 January 1972. Back (L-R) secretary Neil Smith, Freddie Neild, Bobby
Noble, Bobby Neild. Front: Davy Johnston, Chic Allan, trainer Hamish Munro

Drybrough Cup final 1978. Nairn St Ninian lost 0-4 to St Machar at Borough Briggs. Back (L-R) Grant Fraser, Willie Gilmour, Ian Taylor, Dave Grant, Ian Hendry, Ray Sharp, Brian Mackenzie, Jeff Mackintosh, David Fraser, George Fraser, Andy Donaldson, Keith MacMillan, Dave Proctor, Davy Johnston, Gordon T Main, Gordon J Main. Front: John Dick, Doug McLean, Ross Macdonald, Doug Storm, Ian Riddell, Billy Schonewille (mascot), Willie Barron, Colin Cummings, Jim Ness, Harry Schonewille, Jock Willox (president), Donald Wilson

St Ninian FC team 1984-85. Back (L-R) Scott Logan, Stan Brown, Rab Cleland, Ian Hendry, Ronnie Sharp, Alan Armour, Scott Sutherland, Davy Johnston (manager). Front: George Fraser, Ian Petrie, Ritchie Ewan, Eric Robertson (president), Keith Macleod, Graham Ogston, Doug Storm

Proud Scot. A young Davy in his kilt. Perhaps this photo was taken in his bedroom. See below

Davy Johnston's house: a recent pic of Dale Gillespie (No 13) scoring for Nairn in a 5-1 rout of Huntly on 14 August 2010 in a Highland League match at Station Park. In the background (left) is the bedroom window of the house where Davy grew up at 1 Anne Crescent. The window provided a grandstand view for Davy and his family to watch events unfold on the pitch across the road

'Scottish' side, and I don't mean one full of foreign imports, genuinely offers a serious threat to opponents on the European and world stage.

On the cinder slopes of Hampden at the Celtic end at the Scottish Cup final stood a founder member of Nairn St Ninian Junior Football Club. Not for a moment did George Duffy think that on the hallowed turf that day was a future manager of the club he helped to form.

A retired banker, Duffy was brought up in Merryton Crescent, another council estate about a mile from Davy's home in Queenspark. George's uncle, Jock Willox, was a stalwart of St Ninian. In his younger days, along with a neighbour in Merryton Crescent, Mike Mackay, George often met up with Davy for kickabouts at the Riverside and Viewfield football pitches:

'Even then I remember watching in amazement at how Davy could bend the ball from a free-kick like a banana and how easily he could strike the ball with the outside of his feet,' said George. 'The only players we ever saw do that were the Brazilians on television when they won the World Cup in Sweden in 1958.'

In his days at Millbank School with Davy, who was a couple of years his senior, George recalls that, as the school sports day approached, the pupils would organise relay races round the school building. 'If you were in Davy's team you were sure to win because he was the fastest boy in the school,' he recalled. 'I can still picture him racing round the corner on the home stretch with baton in hand.'

George, Robbie Mackay and his brother Mike were all members of a very talented basketball team in Nairn but tragedy struck when the two Mackay brothers, who ran a family licensed grocers in the High Street, were killed in a car accident attending a Hibs-Celtic football match.

Davy could not have asked for a better start to his Pittodrie career. Turnbull had not really fulfilled his promise not to pitch him into the first team before he was ready. But from his debut against Stirling Albion on 17 December he became an automatic first-choice player, culminating in a Hampden final appearance before 126,102 spectators. Joint top-scorers at Pittodrie that season with twenty goals were Jimmy Wilson (from 47 games) and Jimmy Smith (from 45 games). Ernie Winchester's goal haul was seventeen from 29 games, including three as a substitute.

Davy now had a summer tour of America and Canada to look forward to. And while the long trip was an unforgettable experience for the entire squad, Davy sustained what at one stage appeared a career-threatening injury. And Celtic's victory in the European Cup vacated their place in the European Cup-Winners' Cup, which Aberdeen would willingly fill.

The USA and Canada Adventure

Sitting at his home in George Wilson Road, Auldearn, months before his death Davy Johnston relived one of the most fantastic experiences of his life – that summer tour of 1967 on the other side of the Atlantic.

I know now as we sat chatting in his front room that Davy's health prognosis was not good. But I remember that conversation. Reminiscing about what he described as the 'adventure of a lifetime' brought a smile to his face and to mine. As a twelve-year-old in 1967, I had followed every kick of the ball as this unique experiment Stateside was covered extensively in the sporting columns of the UK press.

It is remarkable to think that in eight short months Davy had been catapulted from the obscurity of the Highland League to a Scottish Cup final appearance against the greatest Scottish team ever, and a glamour tournament where he would meet some household names in international football, including England World Cup keeper Gordon Banks, plus Northern Ireland and Scotland legends Derek Dougan and Jim Baxter. And despite his own personal reservations, his scoring exploits in his short spell at Pittodrie gave cause for optimism that Johnston's undoubted talent would begin at last to realise its full potential.

Each team on the tour was adopted by an American city. Aberdeen played as the 'Washington Whips'. President Lyndon Johnston gifted the President's Cup to the winners and Eddie Turnbull, accompanied by his doctor Hugh Falconer, flew over a day after the official party had left Aberdeen airport. Turnbull and some of the organisers of the tournament were introduced to the President at the White House on 25 May – the day Celtic were crowned kings of Europe by beating Inter-Milan in Lisbon.

The Aberdeen manager watched the opening game before flying home for further convalescence. Other British and Irish sides in the competition included Stoke City, Wolves, Hibs, Glentoran, Sunderland, Shamrock Rovers and Dundee United. Teams from Uruguay, Italy, Brazil and Holland were also invited to compete.

Seven weeks after their opening match, Aberdeen met Wolves in the final in Los Angeles. The Dons were reduced to ten men when Smith was sent off, and with the sides locked together at 5-5 after a period of extratime, the game continued and defender Ally Shewan, who finished his playing days with Elgin City, put through his own goal.

Another aspect to Davy was to emerge in a conversation I had later with Gordon Main, a young fan and neighbour of Davy in Nairn who was on the committee of St Ninian with me when Johnston was our manager. Gordon was the same age as myself, thirteen years younger than Davy. He lived just around the corner in Ann Crescent. Gordon revealed to me that during the tour of America, Davy sent a postcard to him from the White House in Washington after the Aberdeen players were given a tour of the seat of power.

Another to receive a card was my next-door neighbour, Mike McPherson, who like me was a signed up member to the DJ fan-club. Mike's father Ian was also a long-serving member on the committee at Station Park. Even though Davy was now in the 'big time', he remembered his roots and his friends. There is no one better to give an account of the glorious summer than Davy himself.

And he did so in an exclusive interview with former Highland League referee Frank Phillips, who also happened to be the editor of *The Football Times*, an Inverness-based Saturday sports paper which competed for readers with the very popular Aberdeen-based *Green Final*. Both papers sadly succumbed to the harsh realities of economic pressures and ever-dwindling advertising revenues.

Frank Phillips' interview about the US adventure gives a flavour of the pleasure Davy took from this, his first trip abroad. He described it as 'the perfect end to a great debut season'. The players, Davy recalled, were raring to go 'like schoolboys at the end of term'. They flew from Heathrow and stayed in Washington at the plush Washington Hilton Hotel. Their first opponents, Stoke City, wore the mantle of Cleveland Stokers and were based in Cleveland, Ohio. They were in Washington for Aberdeen's opening game on 26 May.

The first shock for the players was the state of the playing surface at the DC Stadium, where Stoke won 2-1. The match was played on a baseball ground and, with a surface that was a mixture of grass and blaize, conditions were not suited to skilful players (the west of Scotland generally and Glasgow in particular had a monopoly on blaize pitches, shale surfaces of salmon pink which rutted in cold winter mornings and turned to quicksand in the rain).

'That's no excuse for the fact we lost, because Stoke had to cope with the same problems,' Davy admitted. 'Another feature to emerge from the tour was that rarely did we play before crowds of more than 10,000,' another indication of the difficulties soccer administrators were having in promoting the sport against the pulling power of baseball, which could regularly pull in crowds of 90,000.

Even today, referees come under intense scrutiny in the UK but the referees in this tournament lacked experience and weren't up to speed on the laws of the game. Davy described how experienced professional play-ers from England and Scotland took full advantage, and many of the games turned into bruising encounters with a 'crime rate' and orderings off which would have given SFA blazers sleepless nights.

On the tour, much of which was spent in aeroplanes, given the vast distances, Davy met former Inverness Thistle keeper Ian Crawford in Toronto. Ian played for Toronto in the North American League and they had a chat about old times.

The hotel in Washington, he recalled, was like a palace with 2,500 rooms, a TV in each, and heated swimming pools. The players, he said, played hard on the field and even harder off it.

Sunderland included Jim Baxter, fresh from his memorable 'keepie uppie' demonstration against England that April at Wembley, and he was certainly out for a good time, said Davy: 'I can tell you they enjoyed their trip to America more than some. The antics even stretched to football in the hotel corridors.'

The Dons, though, had departed from Dyce airport under strict instructions from no-nonsense Mr Turnbull: 'You will be representing Aberdeen and Scotland in an international competition. Bear that in mind at all times and act as you would at home.' Davy said the Aberdeen play-ers responded, and locals were in awe of the strict training they under-went as they were put through their paces by Davie Shaw. It was this pro-fessionalism and dedication which took them all the way to the final.

Financially, Davy and his team-mates received a daily allowance of ten dollars, a win bonus of twenty, and ten dollars for a draw. This was not as good as it sounds, for in the summer of 1967 £1 bought US$2.80. In other words, one dollar was worth only around 36p, in today's money, about half what it would fetch today. Nevertheless, apart from their opening defeat by Stoke, the Dons normally picked up a match bonus of some kind. In the sectional leagues the Whips' record was P12, W5, D5, L2, F19, A11, Pts 15 (their second and shock defeat was against Boston Shamrock Rovers). Meanwhile, their wages from Aberdeen were being kept for them until their return.

The Washington Whips' officials said the Aberdeen team were on a $2,000 team winning bonus in the final. Even after their dramatic defeat by Wolves, the players were promised they would receive their bonus, but it's not clear if it was ever received.

Davy recalled one amusing incident during their stay in Washington, although for Aberdeen chairman Charles Forbes it wasn't very funny. Each morning he would walk to the Washington Whips offices to pick up the team's cash allowance and match bonuses: 'It wasn't far, so he enjoyed a morning constitutional except on one occasion,' said Davy. 'He [Mr Forbes] was on his way back with the cash in a small wallet. He'd almost reached the hotel when there was a commotion behind him. He turned to see a 6ft-plus black man bearing down on him, followed by a burly cop brandishing a revolver and shouting. Mr Forbes got the fright of his life. At first he thought the black man was after him, knowing he had a wad of money. When he saw the policeman he thought "What if he shoots?" Anyway, Forbes ducked into the hotel and told us in between gasps of breath of the affair that had us in stitches.'

When he got over the initial shock, the club chairman too saw the funny side of it. But nobody ever found out what happened to the man who was being pursued by the gun-toting cop.

It was six games into the tour that Davy suffered an injury against Uruguayan side Cerro from Montevideo, who were masquerading as the 'New York Skyliners'. It was a 'home' game, which meant it was played in Washington. Davy described the injury as the worst of his career. Playing at outside-right, he gathered a through ball from Francis Munro. With his team already 1-0 in front, Davy had visions of making it 2-0 for the Dons. But the boot of Cerro's left-back caught him on the leg and he went down. The antics of some of today's strikers when they launch themselves to the turf when a defender got the slightest touch on them was something which Davy abhorred. If he took a knock he would do his best to get to his feet and shake it off. But there was no getting up from this challenge:

'I had a gash over seven inches long that eventually needed 25 stitches. I was in terrible pain. We all thought the leg was badly broken but at the time nobody could tell, with all the blood pouring out. The club had been given the services of a first-class doctor. He was the man who turned what seemed likely to be a season out of football into a mere three-week lay-off.'

Davy recalled the physician's name was Dr Resta. He operated on the wound the same day and two days' recuperation in hospital followed. Later he told Davie Shaw that if it had happened in this country 'I would not have kicked a ball again for at least a season'. He explained that the new drugs in use at this time in America were not available in this country [the UK].

As it turned out, Davy was back training within fourteen days. During his recovery in a Washington hospital his wife Margaret heard conflicting versions of the incident through press reports filed by Dons players in British newspapers. At the time, Davy was writing a column on the trip for the *Daily Mail* and Harry Melrose for the *Scottish Daily Express*. Ally

Shewan took over Davy's role and reported the fact he was in hospital but Harry, not wanting to upset Margaret, left out the bit about the hospital.

Margaret read both articles and didn't know what to believe, so she arranged for Aberdeen to lay on a trans-Atlantic phone call to find out the truth. Davy recalled: 'I was feeling pretty fed up but the chat across the Atlantic bucked me up no end, and at least Margaret now knew the exact position.'

During Davy's enforced absence, Aberdeen continued to do the club and Scotland proud by marching all the way to the final on 14 July – a Battle of Britain – and manager Turnbull wasn't going to miss out on seeing it. He had in fact returned to the US some weeks earlier. The final was scheduled for Los Angeles. After intensive therapy and training Davy was deemed fit – testimony indeed to his resilience and the skills of his doctors: 'How I managed to be fit enough in such a short time, I'll never know. Looking back I am glad I didn't miss the grand finale.'

The final was one game which remained vivid in Dave's memory as he recalled how, on one of the hottest days of the tour, Wolves, with Northern Ireland legend Derek Dougan leading their front line, shared a goal-feast. It was 1-1 at half-time and 4-4 after 90 minutes, Jens Petersen laying on a free-kick for Francis Munro to head Aberdeen's fourth goal in the dying seconds of normal time. In extra-time Wolves nosed again once more, only for Munro to level yet again – this time from a penalty, scored 60 seconds after Wolves had missed one themselves. The match then went to a sudden death play-off in the gruelling heat, and six minutes later a deflection off Ally Shewan caught his own keeper Bobby Clark unawares. The own-goal gave Wolves a 6-5 victory and decided the outcome of what had been a marathon adventure for Aberdeen FC.

But it was a game where Davy witnessed the ugliest side of professional football, when his team-mate 'Jinky' Smith retaliated and was sent off after being spat upon by David Wagstaffe, the Wolves winger: 'It was the first time I had encountered this filthy form of fouling,' Davy told Frank Phillips.

Reflecting on the trip overall, Davy said with the money, the sights they had seen, and the pleasure trips, the tour had certainly been the trip of a lifetime: 'Skipper Ally Shewan and the Dons' top officials had been to the White House, and Ally made several TV appearances.'

As for his thoughts on the American fans, Davy didn't really think they understood the game and were bewildered by the intricacies of our national sport.

Among the photographs I received in my research from Davy's son Trevor was one newspaper pic of Davy and Ally Shewan relaxing by the poolside at their luxurious hotel in Washington. There was no designer swimwear or bevy of beautiful women splashed across the tabloid press, as so often emerges from trips abroad involving young football stars today. It was a simple 'holiday' snap of working-class guys relaxing in the sun beside the pool, enjoying living-it-up in a lap of luxury that neither had ever experienced before. They didn't even have sunbeds. Stripped to the waist, the players were wearing trousers rolled up to their knees. The only thing that was missing were the knotted handkerchiefs on their heads. I suspect even sun-block would have been unheard of, and the picture spoke volumes.

Pat Wilson, a Dons fringe player who had arrived from Dunfermline, was one of the sixteen players on the tour. Pat only played a handful of first-team games in two and half seasons with the Dons. He was in the squad for the Scottish Cup final but was omitted on the day. But Wilson played eleven games in the USA (four of them as substitute) and even had the distinction of scoring against England World Cup keeper Gordon Banks, who was on the tour with his club, Stoke City:

'When I was told I was in the squad for America I told Eddie that my fiancee Eirne and I had planned our wedding for 24 June. With Eddie, football came first and he told me I would just have to rearrange the wedding, so it was brought forward to 8 May. It's no secret Eddie didn't suffer fools gladly. Unfortunately, I would go to pieces when I got in the first team and never established myself at the club. But there's no doubt Eddie was ahead of his time as a manager. There was a lot of talk about Jock Wallace's regime at Rangers, putting his players through the mill at the Gullane sands. Eddie had been doing the same before with Aberdeen on the dunes at Balmedie beach.

'Locals will view Balmedie as a place of great tranquility and natural beauty. For me, my memories of Balmedie are of the tortuous sessions our trainer Davie Shaw would put us through until we were on our knees with exhaustion. I had signed for Jock Stein at Dunfermline and he was a different kettle of fish to Eddie. He was a great man-manager. He would ask how my father and my mother were doing. With Eddie, he was totally focused. Football was all he talked about and small talk wasn't on his agenda. He scared the life out of me, but as a tactician he was right up there with Stein.'

Pat Wilson agreed that the trip to the States was a fantastic experience for everyone. But there was one incident he recalls with Davy which gave an insight into the mindset of the shy, unassuming young man from Nairn: 'There we were, lording it, sitting at the poolside of this opulent five-star hotel and Davy remarked: "Well the lads at the laundry will be having their 'piece' now." I replied, "Well Davy, my dad [who was a miner] will be down the pit at Blairhall but that's the last thing I'm thinking about at the moment."

'To me it summed Davy up. He was more concerned about his old pals at the laundry where he worked back in Nairn than savouring the moment for what it was – a brief holiday, living in the lap of luxury, playing a sport we loved.'

Pat Wilson was a winger and although he had a good turn of speed he said Davy was 'the complete package whose pace was explosive'. Pat was moved on by Turnbull in 1968 to Raith Rovers to join manager Tommy Walker, who had brought Johnston to Hearts when he was just sixteen. Years later Pat returned to Aberdeen for a testimonial dinner at the Treetops Hotel for long-serving goalkeeper Bobby Clark:

'I was manager of Cowdenbeath at the time and a few of us were in the men's room and Martin Buchan turned to Eddie and said: "You know, we were all frightened of you." Eddie replied: "Aye, maybe I've changed." I still see him occasionally and he has mellowed – well a wee bit anyway.'

On the team's return to Scotland it was no surprise where Davy headed first – back north to Nairn for a fortnight's holiday with his family. Keen to get back to full fitness for the rigours of a new season after the bad injury he sustained in America, there was always going to be a warm welcome for him from his former team-mates who were beginning their pre-season training at Station Park.

Wrecking Fergie's Title Dream

The serious injury he sustained in America was just a foretaste of things to come in Davy Johnston's second season with the Dons. After starting the first four League Cup group games, he broke a toe at the end of August, which kept him out of the remaining two and also the first three league fixtures. All told, he was out for a month, the first time he was absent from Aberdeen's starting eleven since bursting into the side the previous December. A throat infection saw him sidelined for one game in November, and then he had another three-week lay off in December. Despite these absences, by the end of the season he finished as the club's top scorer on fourteen goals from 36 league and cup appearances.

Despite some good outfield and defensive play, Turnbull was frustrated by his misfiring forward line. He had high hopes for one of his biggest signings, Jim Storrie, who came to Pittodrie in February 1967 from Don Revie's Leeds for a fee of £12,500. At the end of September

Storrie was missing from the squad to travel to play Morton. The official line from Pittodrie was the striker was unfit. But on the day of the match Storrie claimed in the *Press & Journal* he wasn't unfit and he had been made a scapegoat for the previous week's defeat by Clyde. Johnston had recovered from his toe injury and took Storrie's place.

Storrie was consigned to reserve football, where he began scoring prolifically. He put in a transfer request and played only another handful of first-team games before Tommy Docherty snapped him up for Rotherham at the end of December. Docherty had resigned as manager of Chelsea in October and remembered Storrie scoring for the Dons in a pre-season friendly victory over Chelsea at Pittodrie.

Because of their lack of goals, Aberdeen were wallowing in mid-table for most of the 1967-68 season. But Turnbull succeeded in turning their fortunes around in the spring to secure fifth place in the league and a much-coveted slot in Europe for the second year running.

Of Johnston's goals that year, none were more important than the two he saved for the last game of the season. Little did Davy know it at the time, but he had dashed the title aspirations of a footballer who was later to become arguably the greatest British football manager of all time. Aberdeen needed victory at Ibrox to qualify for the European Inter-Cities Fairs Cup. Rangers needed victory to realistically have any chance of wresting the championship from arch rivals and all-conquering Celtic.

Johnston scored two goals and laid on the winner for Ian Taylor in Aberdeen's 3-2 victory in Glasgow. Alex Ferguson, who had signed for Rangers at the start of the season for £60,000 from Dunfermline, was in the Rangers line-up that day, eager to get his hands on a championship badge. Fergie scored to put Rangers 2-1 ahead, but their eventual defeat was largely down to Johnston and Taylor.

In his own autobiography *Managing My Own Life*, Alex admits that he would forget his own name before that decisive Saturday fades from his memory. In one of the press cuttings of this match, I saw a picture of Davy scrambling the ball over the line past Erik Sorensen in goal. In the background was the forlorn figure of Rangers skipper John Greig.

The prospects for Aberdeen's 1967-68 campaign had been given a boost when a 29,000 home crowd watched the Dons beat Docherty's London aristocrats Chelsea. Household names like John Hollins, Ron Harris, Peter Osgood and Scots Eddie McCreadie and Charlie Cooke were in the Chelsea line-up. But a late strike by Jimmy Wilson gave the Dons a 2-1 victory. Johnston was prominent for the Dons but unlucky not to get on the scoresheet. Tambling had put Chelsea ahead in 48 minutes and Storrie equalised before Wilson's 82nd-minute winner.

A League Cup group tie at Pittodrie against Rangers was enough to whet the appetite of supporters for the start of the new season and Storrie was again on target to cancel out an Orjan Persson strike for the Gers. A crushing 0-5 defeat by Dundee United at Tannadice followed, with all the goals coming in the second half. In the next match, at Ibrox, Rangers cruised to a 3-0 win with Johnston an early casualty with a broken toe.

A 2-2 draw with Dundee United sealed the Dons' fate in the competition and Johnston's injury would keep him out of the club's first sojourn in Europe, the Cup-Winners' Cup, when they crushed Icelandic amateurs RFK Reykjavik 10-0 at Pittodrie and 4-1 in Iceland.

Johnston didn't return to the side until 30 September, when Storrie, who had eight goals to his credit since the start of the season, was left out of the team to play Morton. Two late goals saved the Dons' blushes in a 3-3 draw, but Johnston escaped criticism because of his long lay-off. He was back on form with two goals in a 6-0 league trouncing of Dundee United on 16 October. The Dons continued to blow hot and cold and Johnston missed a game against Hibs with a throat infection.

Davy made his European debut against Standard Liège in Belgium on 29 November, but the Dons came home with their tails between their legs after a 0-3 defeat. Turnbull remained upbeat that they could turn the tie around at Pittodrie. Johnston was unwell in training and missed the return leg which the Dons won 2-0, with the Liège players breathing a sigh of relief when the final whistle was sounded.

Three days later Aberdeen signed George Murray from Motherwell and Jimmy Wilson went to Fir Park as part of the deal. Johnston's latest absence kept him out of contention until 23 December for a match at Broomfield against Airdrie.

By the end of the month, Storrie's wish to leave Pittodrie was granted. Southend United had been courting him, but it was back to Yorkshire he went, joining Tommy Docherty at Rotherham. Davy took over the No 9 shirt for a while.

Aberdeen's 0-1 defeat at Airdrie and a 1-4 loss to title-chasing Rangers at Pittodrie brought 1968 to a close. Johnston lifted Aberdeen's spirits with a goal in 40 seconds against Dundee on a bone-hard Dens Park pitch on New Year's Day. An own-goal by Jim Easton completed the scoring. Aberdeen's 2-0 win that day was their first away league victory in Scotland since beating Hearts ten months previously.

A few days later Francis Munro departed for Wolves for £50,000 and with just sixteen points from eighteen league games the Dons had a lot of ground to make up if they were to contend for a European place.

They scraped through against Raith 1-0 in a replayed Scottish Cup-tie and then Johnston and his team-mates rallied to win three league games on the trot before going out of the cup 1-2 to the eventual winners of the trophy, Dunfermline.

The inconsistent form resurfaced and a 0-1 defeat by Partick at Pittodrie was followed by a 1-4 reverse against Celtic. Johnston's consolation goal did little to appease the fans, and worse was to follow when Aberdeen lost 1-3 the following week against Raith in Kirkaldy. A 5-0 win over Hibs gave Aberdeen an outside chance of a place in Europe and the *Press & Journal* reported that Johnston lit the fuse that day, scoring after just nine minutes. He added a second, almost on his knees as he did so, and the *P&J* said the goals would have restored Johnston's confidence after a season plagued by injury.

In April, Davy scored in a 1-1 draw with Kilmarnock at Pittodrie and although narrowly beaten 0-1 by Celtic, victories over St Johnstone and Airdrie gave them a fighting chance of a place in Europe. But it was going to be a tall order.

Their last game was at Ibrox, where Rangers needed victory to keep alive their hopes of the championship. Alex Ferguson was at centre-forward for a Rangers side desperate to wrest the title from Celtic, who had the same number of points with one game to play but enjoyed a much better goal-average. Already, Davy White's side were reeling from a Scottish Cup quarter-final defeat by Hearts and by Leeds in the Fairs Cup. But the Dons had a big incentive themselves and Johnston was in no mood to be charitable. Davy scored twice that day, 27 April, and set up the decisive third goal for Ian Taylor in the last minute of a pulsating game to give the Dons a 3-2 victory.

Rangers were until then unbeaten home and away in the league all season. That they were to lose the championship on the final hurdle must have been gut-wrenching for the players and their supporters. Much to Rangers' chagrin, their own achievement a year earlier in 1967 of reaching the final of the European Cup-Winners' Cup, losing 0-1 to Bayern Munich, went largely unnoticed. In the words of their great winger Willie Johnston, Celtic came home to a heroes' welcome after their Lisbon triumph, but 'we came home to one man and his dog'. So before a ball was even kicked at Ibrox the stage was set for a classic and Turnbull had his side primed well and ready for action.

The match was hailed by sportswriter Norman Macdonald in the following Monday's *Press & Journal* as an Ian Taylor-Dave Johnston inspired spectacular. 'A Day to remember for Dons – And Rangers cannot afford to forget it,' screamed the headlines. Turnbull selected Tommy Craig in preference to Ian Taylor at outside-left with Taylor having to settle for a place on the bench. Rangers fielded Alex Willoughby at inside-right in preference to Andy Penman, who finished off his playing career at Inverness Caley where he, like Davy, became a Highland League legend.

Before an Ibrox crowd of 40,000, former Aberdeen star Dave Smith had the home supporters in raptures in the seventeenth minute when he took a short free-kick from Willie Henderson and drilled the ball past Aberdeen keeper Bobby Clark from 25 yards. But Johnston was in the mood and he levelled the match at 1-1 in 29 minutes. Erik Sorensen, who had a stinker of a game, failed to hold Johnston's shot from a Billy Little pass, and Davy pounced on the loose ball himself and walked it across the line.

Alex Ferguson, who was his club's top scorer that season with 23 goals, was on target to put Rangers 2-1 in front in the 56th minute with a headed goal from a cross from Willie Henderson. But two minutes later and the sides were level pegging again. 'Jinky' Smith went on a mesmerising run down the right and, when Sorensen failed to hold his low shot, who was on hand to scramble the ball across the line when it came back off the post but Johnston? In the 62nd minute Turnbull made an inspired substitution when he replaced Tommy Craig with Ian Taylor. In the 89th minute Johnston made a blistering run from the halfway line to the corner flag, where he crossed low and hard for Taylor to apply the *coup de grâce* with a first-time drive with the outside of the boot. Despite Rangers being twice in front, match commentators acknowledged Aberdeen were fearless as they went about their business and finished deserved winners. Sir Alex, in his own autobiography *Managing My Own Life*, describes how the legions of Rangers fans packed the stadium to overflowing. Everything had been going according to script when Dave Smith nudged Rangers ahead with the first goal of the game. Alex said a second goal looked on the cards, only for Sorensen's blunder to let Johnston in for the equaliser, and the Rangers keeper's nervy afternoon continued.

After his headed goal, Ferguson claimed Aberdeen had a let off when he was pulled down by Dons centre-half Tommy McMillan in the box, with no penalty awarded, but when Johnston's second goal squirmed through Sorensen's hands for Aberdeen's second equaliser, and Ian Taylor rammed home the winning goal from Davy's cross, Rangers supporters steamed for the exits, knowing the game, their unbeaten record, and the title were all gone.

Angry fans milled around the main exit at Ibrox for hours after the final whistle, dressing room windows were smashed and the players had to be kept indoors until the trouble died down. In all the fuss, it has been largely forgotten that even had Rangers beaten Aberdeen, Celtic would still have pipped them for the championship. Following Rangers' defeat, Celtic needed to lose by sixteen goals to Dunfermline four days later to concede the title on goal-average. Instead Celtic won 2-1.

Nevertheless, Davy's two goals at Ibrox left him as Aberdeen's leading scorer that season with fourteen goals, one ahead of Jinky Smith.

Johnston added two more goals, for good measure, the following week when Eddie Turnbull took the Dons to play Nairn County at Station Park in a friendly as part of the deal struck when the player was transferred to Pittodrie eighteen months earlier. Among the cuttings passed to me by Davy's son Trevor for my research into this book was a photograph from this match in one of the daily papers. It was a snap which to me epitomises why we all love this game so much.

It shows Davy scrambling home the second Ibrox goal after the ball came back off Sorensen's left-hand post. Davy is a couple of feet from the line, while in the background looking on in utter despair is Rangers skipper John Greig – he knew the title was slipping through his fingers.

Something that strikes me as being unusual about this match are the two goals Davy scored. Anyone who witnessed him play will remember him for his blistering speed and goals scored from twelve, twenty, 30, aye even 40 yards – but here were two in one game from inside the six-yard box. It was just another string to his bow. He could be a poacher as well, and he was as adept at snapping up morsels, breathing down the goal-keeper's neck, as he was banging them in from the edge of the box and beyond.

Perhaps this was Davy's finest hour in an Aberdeen shirt. Sadly, the next season with the Dons was to be his last – not because he wasn't wanted at Pittodrie. But the pull of home was too great.

Relegation Worries

By one of those ironies, Aberdeen would still have finished fifth and secured their place in the Fairs Cup if they had drawn at Ibrox. Yet few could have forecast the nightmare season 1968-69 would become.

From finishing fifth with 37 points from 34 games the previous season, Aberdeen struggled to find their form and the threat of relegation loomed large over Pittodrie for most of the campaign. They finished in a lowly fifteenth place with just 26 points from 34 games, ahead of Raith Rovers on 21 and doomed Falkirk (18 points) and Arbroath (16).

It was a turbulent time for the club and for Eddie Turnbull who, try as he might, couldn't get his team out of the doldrums. It was a season when he dropped Scotland international goalkeeper Bobby Clark and received a transfer request from one of his rising stars, Martin Buchan. To Turnbull's credit, even in adversity he was always looking to the future. He dissuaded young Buchan from moving from Pittodrie, and the following season Martin became the youngest ever captain to lift the Scottish Cup when, at 21, he led the Dons to a 3-1 victory over Celtic at Hampden Park. Had Davy stayed he could well have been part of that triumph. Turnbull also had his sights on a certain striker down Greenock way who was to write his name in Pittodrie folklore and scored from the penalty spot in that final – Joe Harper.

The only highlight for Aberdeen in 1968-69 was a Scottish Cup run which took them to the semi-finals, only to crash to an embarrassing 1-6 defeat by a Rangers side no doubt still smarting from having their championship hopes snatched from their grasp at Ibrox by the Dons on the last day of the 1967-68 season.

In fact, during that April weekend when Aberdeen had snuffed out Rangers' title hopes, Turnbull stayed on in Glasgow rather than travel home with his triumphant players. He was set to buy centre-forward Jim Forrest from Preston North End for £25,000 and Partick Thistle winger Tommy Rae for £20,000.

As Turnbull wrote in his autobiography, 'I decided we needed a proven goalscorer.' Some might say he already had one, Davy Johnston, the club's top scorer in the season just finished. Turnbull evidently felt differently. Johnston to date had the distinction of never being dropped in the season and a half since his introduction. The few matches he had missed had all been down to injury or illness. For the start of 1968-69, however, he was left out. For a player low on self-esteem to start with, this cannot have improved Davy's fragile confidence. It would be a long season for Johnston as well as for Aberdeen.

Jim Forrest, who had been dumped by Rangers after the debacle of their 1967 Scottish Cup exit at Berwick, had endured an unhappy time at Deepdale, failing to score in sixteen outings. Some Aberdeen fans questioned Turnbull's judgment in opting for Forrest when the striker had appeared to lose his scoring touch.

On the other hand, Tommy Rae had scored nineteen goals in 42 games for the Firhill club and he seemed a safe bet. In fact, the reverse proved to be the case. By the end of the season Forrest had 23 goals to his credit from 47 appearances. Rae, on the other hand, only scored once in sixteen appearances for his new club. Johnston's tally was nine from 33, plus two substitute appearances. All but one of those nine goals were scored from the wing. Davy wore the No 9 shirt just three times all season, the last of which was in January 1969. His days as an out-and-out Aberdeen centre-forward were over. But did Turnbull have plans to use him in a different capacity?

The season got off to a dreadful start with a 1-4 defeat at Shawfield by Clyde in the League Cup group. A 1-0 win over Dunfermline, followed by a 4-1 win over Dundee United (both at Pittodrie) raised hopes the Dons could qualify from their section for the knock-out stages. It was not to be, however. Although the Dons won 2-1 at East End Park, further defeats by Clyde (0-2 at Pittodrie) and Dundee United (0-1 at Tannadice) ended their interest in the competition, with Clyde going through.

When the league campaign got under way in September, Aberdeen threw away a point in their first outing at Dens Park when Dundee came from two down to lead 4-2 before a Dons rally earned a 4-4 draw. Wretched form continued to manifest itself and, before their first meeting of the season with Rangers at Ibrox on 26 October, Aberdeen had accumulated just three points from seven games, losing their last five.

The Dons raised their game in Govan. Johnston had been recalled earlier at the expense of the disappointing Rae, and he fired the Dons into the lead after three minutes. Then Forrest, determined to prove the Gers were wrong to offload him after the Berwick fiasco, chipped in with a double. The Rangers fans chanted for substitute Alex Ferguson to come on and, after replacing Sandy Jardine, Fergie made an immediate impact, reducing the leeway to 3-1 with seven minutes left. Willie Henderson added a second but the damage was done and Aberdeen travelled home with much-needed points from their second successive 3-2 win at Ibrox.

On the European front, Aberdeen earned a 0-0 draw against Slavia Sofia on 17 September, and two weeks later booked their place in the second round with a 2-0 home win before 29,000 spectators at Pittodrie.

Johnston figured in neither of those games. He did play, however, in the first leg of the second round against Spanish side Real Zaragoza three days before the victory at Ibrox, but found himself out in the cold for the return match in Spain, although he was in the travelling party. In the home leg, goals from Forrest and Smith had Aberdeen in a commanding position before Zaragoza, winners of the competition in 1964, were given a lifeline after Tommy McMillan slashed Lapetra's cross past Bobby Clark for an own-goal. The 'away' goal rule severely damaged the Dons' prospects. In the final minute a touch-line drive from Johnston could have restored Aberdeen's two-goal advantage but Spanish keeper Nieves made a superb punched clearance.

In the return leg Zaragoza won 3-0, goals from Marcelino (35 minutes) and Tejedor (43) breaking down stubborn Aberdeen resistance. A third goal from Villa on 78 minutes sealed Aberdeen's fate.

The Dons' line-up that night was: Clark, Hermiston Shewan, Petersen, McMillan, Craig, Robb, Smith, Forrest, Buchan, Taylor. Bustling Davie Robb had been chosen at the expense of Johnston – the only change from the side which won the first leg.

On their return to Scotland, Turnbull defended his tactics. He said his side had played the first half defensively and were physically stronger than their opponents, but the second goal just before half-time meant the Dons were up against it.

The losing habit prevailed on the domestic front and a 1-5 defeat by Dunfermline in Fife (when Johnston was substituted) and a 2-6 home thrashing by Hibs (when Johnston was absent) on successive Saturdays saw Turnbull wield the axe. The goalie he had brought with him from Queen's Park, Bobby Clark, was replaced by Ernie McGarr, who went on to be capped for Scotland. For Clark it was to be a long wait before he regained his first-team place. He was restored in February 1970 and was in the side which won the Scottish Cup that year.

After the humbling by Hibs, Airdrie were next up and, with Johnston back on board, Aberdeen's 0-2 defeat at Broomfield saw them sitting on just ten points from fifteen games.

The Scottish Cup brought some respite in the New Year from their league woes. Victory over Berwick (3-0) at Pittodrie in January saw the Dons paired with Cup-holders Dunfermline in the next round. No doubt with their 1-5 league hammering in Fife still fresh in their memories, Aberdeen were out for revenge. After a 2-2 draw at Pittodrie on Tuesday, 25 February, the teams had to replay the following night at East End Park. Davy played in both games, and a double strike from Davie Robb saw Aberdeen through to play Kilmarnock in the quarter-finals, which they won 3-0 after a replay.

Aberdeen's only route to Europe would be via winning the Scottish Cup, and to do that they had first to get past Rangers in the semi-finals. Having already beaten them twice at Ibrox within the past year, there was hope. Johnston seems to have restored his manager's faith in his contribution for he was virtually ever-present on the right wing throughout the last three months of the season. The Parkhead semi-final on 22 March, however, saw Willie Johnston in devastating form. He scored a hat-trick in Rangers' 6-1 triumph.

It wasn't until a midweek match at Pittodrie on 2 April, when they trounced Morton 6-3, that Aberdeen were virtually assured of safety from relegation. Johnston scored two goals that night and a certain Mr Joe Harper was on target for the Cappielow side.

Three days later Johnston scored his last competitive goal for the Dons in a 3-1 home win over Airdrie, and the following Wednesday he was in the Aberdeen side which drew 0-0 with Rangers at Pittodrie, a result which again snuffed out any lingering hopes Rangers might have entertained of winning the championship. Celtic on 54 points finished five points clear of Rangers.

An ignominious 1-1 draw at Clyde, with Jim Forrest snatching a last-minute equaliser on 23 April 1969 brought the curtain down on Davy Johnston's career at Aberdeen.

He had told his wife he would be back in Nairn for his daughter Sharon to start primary school. And he stuck to the pledge he made to himself. Although Johnston played another couple of friendlies for the Dons against Highland League sides Ross County and Peterhead in the weeks which followed, he walked out on the Dons and no amount of persuasion could make him return.

Why I Quit – Davy Johnston

After the trauma Aberdeen had faced in the 1968-69 season, Davy's decision to walk out on the Dons was big news in the sports pages of the Scottish media.

He cited problems caused by a broken nose he suffered years earlier in the clash with Roy Fraser of Inverness Thistle as the reason behind his decision to quit top-flight Scottish football. But it was common knowledge he never settled in the city and his return to the Highlands was as inevitable as it was regrettable for his army of fans who held out such aspirations that Davy would take his rightful place at the top table of Scotland's football elite.

Davy claimed he never adjusted to the rigours of training for a full-time professional club and was often physically sick, a fact borne out later in this book by his best mate at Aberdeen, Ally Shewan.

It was common knowledge that relations between Davy and Eddie Turnbull were sometimes strained, although Turnbull's position remains that he was simply frustrated that such a great talent never fully blossomed into the international player he was undoubtedly capable of becoming. Turnbull told me at the time of Davy's death that he believed – had he got him as a youngster – he could have moulded him into another Bobby Charlton. They were similar players both in stature and ability, said Turnbull, the way they were at ease with the ball on either foot, their striking power, and of course their great vision of all that was going on around them. It was his hope, said Turnbull, to do with Johnston what Manchester United did with Charlton and play him in a deeper role in midfield where, with that great vision and precision passes, he could orchestrate play – sadly it was not to be.

Turnbull was a hard taskmaster and Davy's wife admitted her husband was more sensitive and reacted differently to the demands being placed on him by his manager than other players did. In one interview at the time, pictured with his young son David and daughter Sharon on his knee, he spoke candidly about his shock decision.

Now aged 26, Davy told the *Daily Record*'s Ian Broadley in an interview in his club flat that he had had no row with the Dons and that he had been treated well by the club: 'This is something I have been considering for the past six months. I only held off because the team was struggling. This is my personal decision. I have never fully adjusted to the pace and training of a top side like Aberdeen. I broke my nose when playing in the Highland League and was advised by a medical expert to give up football. However, since joining the Dons I have been plagued with nasal and throat infections and I never felt I had the stamina to maintain consistent form. After a hard game it sometimes took me days to recover. Now I feel my health would suffer by remaining in the top grade of football.'

Johnston had planned to speak to Turnbull to ask for his release, but the manager was away fixing up new young talent recommended to him by chief scout Bobby Calder. Joe Smith, brother of inside-forward Jimmy, Willie Young and Chic McLelland would be new faces coming through the doors of Pittodrie as Johnston went in the opposite direction. Jimmy Smith and Tommy Craig were also exiting Pittodrie, Smith for £80,000 to Newcastle, and Craig, almost nineteen, for £100,000 to Sheffield Wednesday. Davy was quoted in the press saying, with no disrespect to Tommy, no player was worth that kind of money – I wonder what price would be put on a player of Johnston's class today? He even thought the modest renumeration they were receiving in those days – little more than twice the salary of a tradesman – was too much.

Since the beginning of 1969 sports journalists said Johnston had hit a great seam of form, playing out wide, but he was adamant he wanted out: 'If the Dons don't release me, I'm quite prepared to quit football altogether. I cannot continue the way I'm going,' he said.

Margaret recalls the trauma of their move back north. 'The day we left our club house in Aberdeen there were reporters waiting on the doorstep asking Davy why he was quitting. We had the children and our bags and a train to catch and I was very angry. We came back north and we had to stay with my mother in Auldearn, and Sharon went to school in Auldearn. Our furniture was put in storage. Davy was always a hard worker and he had already arranged to get his old job back at the laundry. He wanted to rejoin Nairn and hoped Aberdeen would release him so he could go back to Station Park. But that didn't happen and he ended up going to Caley, where he was reunited with his pal Chic [Allan] and he began to really enjoy his football again.'

Margaret said although Davy had no regrets about joining Aberdeen, he had no regrets about leaving either: 'Once he got something into his head there was no changing his mind. He could be very stubborn. He enjoyed Aberdeen and so did I, but Davy just wanted home. Had it not been for Ally [Shewan], I think Davy would have left earlier. I wanted him to stay. We had a better life there. We were never going to be wealthy like the footballers of today. But we had a better standard of living and could have enjoyed the experience for a lot longer. We came home to nothing. When we were in Aberdeen we got lots of visitors from Nairn, including his mother, Chic, and Tom Walls and Colin Young of Nairn County who often called round when they had been to see Davy play at Pittodrie. Luke Botto, who was a neighbour of Davy's mother in Anne Crescent, was another regular and he would often drive us up to Nairn for the weekend after the match because Davy didn't drive.'

Margaret also revealed that her mother, Jessie Pinder, even enlisted the help of Lisbon Lion Tommy Gemmell to try and persuade Davy to return to the Dons after he broke his contract: 'Tommy Gemmell regularly stayed at the Lion Hotel in Auldearn where my mother worked. He was a great friend of Willie Fraser who owned the hotel and she asked him to have a word with Davy to try and persuade him to go back to Pittodrie. Tommy came round to my mother's house to speak to him but there was no way Davy was going to meet him. He went out to the bingo instead.'

As a regular at Station Park, I lived in the forlorn hope that Davy would get his wish and return to his old stamping ground. But it did not happen – not for another six years, anyway. Sandy Finlayson, the former Nairn County secretary, again takes up the story: 'Aberdeen were looking for a fee for Davy and we knew we couldn't afford him. One day Eric Geddes, the Nairn County trainer, gave me a call to see something that was going on in the railway station car park. There we saw Dave Birrell, the Caley chairman, in his car with Chic Allan speaking to Davy. Chic, of course, had been with Caley since leaving Nairn in 1965 and they had the funds to pay a fee to Aberdeen and he signed for them.'

It is believed Caley paid £2,000 to get him released from his Aberdeen contract – a snip at the price. Davy's career blossomed at Telford Street, where he became a regular fixture in the side. Indeed it even had an adverse impact on Nairn because many fans would travel west on County's matchdays just to watch Davy in action in Inverness – another demonstration of his awesome pulling power.

At the end of this book I list tributes to Davy's talent by his Aberdeen team-mates. But as the curtain comes down on his Pittodrie years, let us take a few soundings. I tried to get a comment from Sandy Jardine and John Greig of Rangers about their recollections of Johnston as an opponent. They were players I admired greatly and both graciously contacted me but said there was little they could remember about Davy. This is puzzling. Professional footballers usually have a keen memory for opponents, particularly those who sparkle against them. All told, Greig faced Davy seven times in Aberdeen v Rangers clashes and Jardine four times. If they don't remember anything about him, perhaps Davy's contribution to the Dons' cause might be overstated. Perhaps, too, if they read this book it will jog their memory.

Kevin Stirling, author of *The Aberdeen Centenary History* and *Aberdeen: Champions of Scotland 1954-55*, was ten years years old when Davy quit Pittodrie in 1969. Kevin says: 'If anything I did not really notice him, in contrast to the likes of Jinky Smith and a young Tommy Craig, who both caught my eye.' This is significant, because dashing centre-forwards and flying wingers are the players most likely to catch the eye of young boys eagerly watching from the terraces. Chris Gavin, former editor of *The Red Final* and now a club director at Pittodrie, was in his mid-teens and tends to agree: 'I know he [Davy] had a pretty good scoring record but my recollection is of a player who was more journeyman than superstar, but a useful part of the Dons' team.'

David Innes has taken a keen interest in the Dons during the Turnbull era. David has stronger memories: 'My recollection is that Johnston played through the middle until Jim Storrie signed from Leeds in 1967. Thereafter, Johnston either played as a twin striker with Storrie or played on the wing opposite Jimmy Wilson. I thought Davy was an excellent player, but perhaps a tad lightweight for the rough and tumble of the First Division then. He seemed fair and perhaps a bit too much of a nice guy when faced with the take-no-prisoners robustness of the likes of Rangers' Ronnie McKinnon and niggly street wisdom of Celtic's Bertie Auld. He had excellent natural ball skills and a great instinct for goal. My outstanding memory of Johnston was in early April 1967 when we beat Falkirk 6-1 at Pittodrie. He tore them apart, scoring a couple himself as

I recall, and impressed the ten-year-old me with his baffling ball control. He was an automatic pick for the squad which toured the US in 1967, ahead of Winchester and others of the first-team squad of the time.'

And what of the verdict of Johnston's manager, Eddie Turnbull? Turnbull's autobiography sends out mixed messages. On the one hand, he devotes a page to Davy, this 'hugely talented player', only to confess that at Aberdeen 'he never hit the heights'. Turnbull even hints that he himself might have been partly responsible. Davy is described as 'a gentle boy', while Turnbull does not deny 'ranting and raving at players' and having 'a fierce air about me'. 'My reputation as a disciplinarian – thoroughly deserved, even though I say so myself – stems from those early days at Aberdeen.' Was Turnbull's managerial ferocity a factor in driving Davy away? Would a more paternalistic manager, in the mould, say, of Arsène Wenger, have got more out of the player? And did such managers exist in the brutal footballing world of the 1960s?

A Highland Homecoming

If anyone wants to question the 'cult' status of Davy Johnston in the north, I suppose a flavour of that was captured in conversations I had with fans of that era on his return to the Highland League. Many Nairn supporters confessed they deserted the terracings of Station Park to watch Johnston performing at Telford Street on a Saturday afternoon. Carloads travelled west along the A96 and I'm sure fans from other parts of the north wanting to see the Highland exile back in action added to attendances at Caley's ground.

In a waiting room at Raigmore Hospital at the time I was writing this book, I passed some time in conversation about football with a gentleman from Dingwall. I knew he would remember the players of that era and without hesitation he said Johnston was the best he had ever seen: 'The truth is there's a lot a players in the Scottish League today who think they are good,' he said, choosing his words carefully. 'The difference is Johnston and many others who were playing in the Highland League at that time *were* good.'

Alan Elder, a cousin of Davy's pal Chic Allan, revealed that Chic was instrumental in getting Davy onto the books at Telford Street: 'Davy was basically kicking his heels and not playing after walking out on Aberdeen. The three of us were out walking up to Firhall [a bridge over the River Nairn] and Chic suggested to Davy he come and join him at Caley. The following week Chic took him through to training.'

With Nairn strapped for cash, there was never any question that they could outbid the Inverness club for Johnston's services. And there's no doubt Dave Birrell, the Caley chairman, and his committee knew it would be money well spent, having a player of the calibre of Johnston on their books.

In 1979 Tom Hart of Hibs shocked the football world when he signed the wayward genius George Best. At 33 his reputation for womanising and boozing had preceded him and he was certainly past his prime. But Best had never lost his box office appeal and even at £2,000 a game he was good value for the Easter Road club, which quadrupled their home attendance when 20,622 turned up for his first game, against Partick Thistle. I'm not saying Johnston had that kind of impact on the gates at Telford Street. But there's no doubt he was a big draw and his signing was a major coup for Caley.

Davy was still only 26 when he signed at the start of the 1969-70 season, and Caley were to get six good years out of Davy before he moved on to finish his Highland League career where it had all begun, at Nairn. In terms of silverware, for Davy these were his most fruitful years in the Highland League. During his spell with Caley he lifted one North Cup, two Highland League Cups and two Qualifying Cup medals, and of course the much-coveted championship in 1970-71, which had eluded him even in the halcyon days when he couldn't break the scoring habit at Nairn a decade earlier.

If any of Caley's opponents harboured hopes that Johnston's controversial departure from Pittodrie may have blunted his appetite for scoring, they were in for a rude awakening. The goals began flowing freely and by the end of his first season he had bagged 52 for his new club – and his partnership with Chic Allan was to become part of Caley folklore. In 188 competitive games for Caley, he was to score 157 goals – unlike his Nairn days, this time we are keeping proper count – and within three months of signing at Telford Street he had added Highland League Cup and Qualifying Cup medals to the North Cup badges he had won with Nairn. But these fine cup runs and qualification for the Scottish Cup were to prove Caley's downfall as far as their title challenge was concerned. They fell well behind in their league programme and, despite a valiant attempt, just failed to make up the ground to give them a play-off chance against Elgin City, who clinched their third successive title and their eighth championship in eleven seasons.

Johnston made his debut for Caley in August 1969 in a friendly at Montrose, which Caley won 1-0. When the season got under way for real, he proved to the fans he had lost none of his scoring touch. He scored two in a 5-3 Highland League Cup first-leg win against local rivals Thistle and followed that up with a hat-trick in the league in midweek against Fraserburgh. On 20 August the two Inverness clubs met at Kingsmills in the second leg and Thistle, leading 2-0 after 90 minutes, took the tie to extra-time. Johnston grabbed the winner and he scored hat-tricks in the a 4-2 victory over Ross County in the quarter-final and in an 8-2 win over Lossie in the semis. Caley beat Peterhead 2-1 in the final at Elgin – both goals scored by Chic Allan.

Johnston also scored the winner in a replayed Qualifying Cup semi with Peterhead in October. The final with Ross County was over two legs the following month and, with the sides inseparable at 1-1 after the first tie at Telford Street, 4,000 fans turned out to watch the showdown at Victoria Park. Caley triumphed 4-1 in the second leg with Johnston (two) Allan and Freddie Neild the scorers. In between their cup exploits, Caley were picking off their opponents in the league and they were unbeaten until the last game of 1969, when they crashed 0-3 to Clach a week after dumping Ross County unceremoniously out of the Scottish Cup, 5-0 in a preliminary round.

Caley easily accounted for Second Division Stranraer, 5-2, in the first round of the national tourney in January, and were drawn away to Motherwell in the next round, where they lost 1-3. The Fir Park side led 2-0 at half-time but a Johnston goal gave visitors Caley a chance of an upset until a late penalty goal for Motherwell put the tie out of their reach.

Their cup exploits resulted in Caley losing ground to Elgin, Ross County and local rivals Thistle in the league race and they were faced with six games in the last sixteen days of the season. Three games from the finishing line, a 4-1 victory over Elgin left them four points behind the Borough Briggs club, who were on 49 points with two to play. Caley's last two games were away to Thistle and Ross County on Wednesday, 13, and Friday, 15 May. Former Elgin centre-forward Willie Grant ill-advisedly made a comment in one newspaper before the match at Kingsmills that Thistle would make sure the title went to his old club and he hoped the championship would not return to the Highland capital without Thistle having won it.

A hat-trick from Allan and a goal from Freddie Neild put Caley on easy street. 'Two cleverly placed goals by Johnston which had the mark of a football artist completed Thistle's discomfiture,' observed one sportswriter.

If anything, Grant's comments only served to fire up the Caley players. But the 6-1 victory at the home of their local rivals had taken its toll.

Caley needed two more points from their game 48 hours later at Dingwall to clinch the title. But they couldn't break through a resolute Ross County defence and a solitary goal gave the home side victory.

That match was played on a Friday night and, had Caley won it, the Highland League would have had to apply to the SFA for a dispensation to extend the season for a play-off between Caley and Elgin. Both teams would have been on 49 points but goal-difference didn't decide the title in those days. It wasn't until after Nairn beat Fraserburgh in a play-off to win the 1975-76 championship that the rules were changed and goal-difference became decisive in the event of teams finishing level on points. Inverness Thistle finished the season in third place, despite having scored a record 124 league goals.

Johnston's quest for a Highland League medal finally ended the following season, 1970-71. Caley not only broke Elgin's stranglehold on the championship, but held off a challenge from Thistle, who had prolific strikers themselves in Ian Stephen and Johnnie Cowie. Thistle finished runners up, but their goals tally of 115 goals surpassed Caley's by 23.

The Kingsmills club reached three cup finals that season, winning only one – the Highland League Cup – beating Clach 6-1 before a crowd of 3,000. Thistle lost in the finals of the North Cup and the revived Inverness Cup – both to Elgin City. Although they never faced the same backlog of fixtures that proved Caley's downfall the previous season, Thistle's cup commitments allowed their town rivals to steal a march on them on the home straight for the championship. Fine side though they were, Thistle couldn't make up the ground and finished five points adrift of Caley when the final curtain came down.

The Telford Street side, in fact, remained unbeaten in the league until 23 January, when they lost 0-3 at Peterhead. They went top of the table in October and, despite valiant attempts by Thistle, Peterhead and Elgin, no one could budge them.

For Davy Johnston it was another free-scoring year, when he clocked up 39 goals in 36 league and cup appearances. One of the highlights was a double hat-trick scored in a 10-1 Qualifying Cup win over Huntly in September. In fact, that Saturday the three Inverness clubs scored 25 goals between them. Brian Munro also scored six in Clach's 10-0 trouncing of Wick Academy, and Johnny Cowie of Thistle was a hat-trickster in a 5-0 win at Forres.

The class of Johnston was never far from the headlines in victory and even in defeat. On Boxing Day, Caley triumphed in a key four-pointer over Thistle at Kingsmills. The *Inverness Courier* reported the match thus: 'On the heavy ground, which was something of a disadvantage to

Thistle's speedier players, Caley's older and more experienced team played a more mature game. It was perhaps not without significance that at the end of the first half, which found players on both sides slithering in the mud, Dave Johnston, the Caley centre-forward, went back to the dressing room with his shorts still spotless. He kept his feet and his head when all around were losing theirs. It was not surprising, then, that it was Johnston's two goals – eighteen and fifteen minutes from the end – which gave Caledonian their valuable victory.' Cumming of Thistle and Allan of Caley were the first-half scorers in Caley's 3-1 win, which opened up a four-point gap at the top of the table.

Later in the 1970-71 season, in February, Thistle knocked Caley out of the Inverness Cup, scoring three without reply. One sportswriter concluded: 'In Johnston, a real schemer whose delicate touches in opening up play, initiating moves, and having a go himself occasionally, stamped-him in a class by himself Caley had a potential match winner.' It is clear from describing Johnston as a 'schemer' that he was no longer employed as an all-out attacker, and that he could create goals as well as score them.

Thistle went on to lose the final 2-4 on aggregate to Elgin, but there were calls for an inquiry after the second leg into the use of 'dangerous or defective studs' after two Thistle players, centre-half Hugh Lazenby and young inside-forward Peter Corbett, required hospital treatment to cuts which required in total 22 stitches. Caley finished the 1970-71 season top with 51 points from 30 games, with Thistle second on 46.

In this era many fine young Inverness players were being blooded by the three Inverness teams – Alan MacLaren, Sandy Cuthbert and Brian McBey from Inverness Royal Academy (IRA) and Peter Corbett from the High School all became established first-team players at Kingsmills, but Corbett later had spells with the other two Inverness clubs and Ross County. Sandy Anderson, Alan Stuart and Kenny MacGregor from the High School and Gordon Fyfe from Inverness Royal Academy played for Caley, while Clach also tapped into the rich seam of local talent, signing Alistair 'Sugar' Kennedy, Alan Stevenson, Billy MacDonald, Bill Nelson from the High School. Walter Wright and Sandy Young from the IRA played for Clach.

I was to get to know Gordon Fyfe well as we both pursued careers in journalism, Gordon with the *Inverness Courier*, then owned by the redoubtable Evelyn Barron, and myself in my home town paper, the *Nairnshire Telegraph*, another independent paper, owned by Alistair Bain. Gordon went on to become north news editor with the *Press & Journal* in Inverness and in 1990 he joined the ranks of the civil service as press officer with Highland Regional Council. He has been the public relations guru for the Regional Council and its successor, Highland Council, for over twenty years. I remember Gordon as a flying winger with Caley and often cursed him as his darting runs and telling crosses ripped through the Nairn defence on more than one occasion during the 1970s. He was just seventeen but played seven games during that title-winning season. Until he was spotted by Caley scouts, however, he had been a lifelong Thistle fan. Gordon's career was cut short when he sustained a compound fracture of his leg in a match at Lossiemouth in April 1979 when he was just 27. But he has fond memories, particularly of his second year with Caley in 1971-72.

The championship that season went deservedly to Thistle, who had been knocking on the door for so long and were the highest scoring team in the league for the fourth year running. Caley in fact played five cup finals on successive Saturdays, which probably merits some explanation.

It all started on 30 October 1971 with a Highland League Cup final against Huntly which went to a replay. The first game was played at Elgin's Borough Briggs, when the partnership of Johnston and Chic Allan pulled the fat out of the fire for Caley, who were 0-2 down after seventeen minutes. A double from Chic and a further goal from Davy put Caley ahead, but Huntly pegged the match back to 3-3 to take the final to a second game. But that would have to wait.

The Qualifying Cup final against Elgin was to take precedence over the next three weeks. In the semi-final, which had gone to a replay, it was again the Johnston-Allan double act which gave Caley victory against Thistle before a 3,000 crowd. Chic scored two and Davy got the third in a comfortable 3-0 win.

The first leg of the Qualifying Cup final was played on 6 November at Telford Street and although it finished goalless the match enthralled the crowd of 2,100. It was a thriller from start to finish and a bruising encounter it turned out to be, as no quarter was given nor asked. Playing in the Elgin side was Johnston's old mate at Pittodrie, Ally Shewan.

The second leg, on 13 November, was always going to be a crowd pleaser and 3,100 paid through the gate at Borough Briggs. The players certainly didn't disappoint. It looked all over with Caley leading 2-1 through goals from Alan Presslie and Chic Allan as the seconds ticked away. But in injury-time substitute Hugh Thom snatched a dramatic equaliser to take the final to a third game.

Caley won the toss for choice of venue and it was still everything to play for when these two giants locked horns again at Telford Street on 20 November. Although Johnston was not among the goals, Fyfe, who came on as a late sub for Freddie Neild, reckons Davy was the outstanding player afield. The pitch was covered in snow at kick-off but it soon disappeared as the sides set about each other at a blistering pace. An Ally Shewan own-goal after five minutes gave Caley the lead and young winger Donald Park, a schoolboy from Lochaber, put Caley two up. Gerry Graham and Tom Corkan got Elgin back on level terms but further goals from the precocious youngster Park and striker Jim Lynas put the tie out of Elgin's reach. Park was to go on and have a fine career in the Scottish League with Hearts.

Caley: Mackenzie, R Neild, Noble, Stapleton, Bennett, Presslie, Park, Allan, Lynas, Johnston, F Neild (Fyfe).

Elgin: Lawtie, Gerrard, Nicol, Gilbert Shewan, Macdonald, Corkan, MacCarthy, MacArthur, Graham, Thom; sub Munro.

There remained, of course, that unfinished business of the Highland League Cup final. Still on a high from their Qualifying Cup success the previous Saturday, there was no stopping Caley this time around as they crushed Huntly 6-1 in the replay at Elgin. Park had two first-half goals and Freddie Neild added a third in the 50th minute before Park completed his hat-trick. Lynas and Stapleton completed the rout before Brownlee snatched a late consolation for Huntly. The first half was described as scrappy in one newspaper: 'but one bright feature was the brilliant play of Dave Johnston on the Caley right wing. Time and again he tore through the Huntly defence to set up chances for his team mates.' Schemer and winger: Caley were certainly exploiting Davy's versatility.

Caley: Mackenzie, R Neild (Macgregor), Noble, Stapleton, Bennett, F Neild, Park, Allan, Lynas, Johnston, Fyfe.

Huntly: Beattie, Watson, Martin, Laws, Reidford, Finnie, Forsyth, Brownlee, Williamson, Cruickshanks, Chalmers (Low).

Apart from the cup finals, Gordon recalled an epic Scottish Cup-tie when Caley beat Thistle 4-3 and went out in the next round 1-3 to Elgin before 5,598 fans at the city ground on 5 February 1972. Gate receipts were £1,147.

Being a newspaperman, Gordon was particularly tickled by one writer who captured the moment with the headline: 'Thom and Gerry play cat and mouse with Caley,' a reference to Elgin strikers Hugh Thom and Gerry Graham, and of course the great cartoon series of that period, *Tom and Jerry*.

Sub-editors at *The Sun* newspaper years later came up with the daddy of all football headlines when they splashed their sports pages with the unforgettable 'Super Caleygoballistic Celtic are atrocious' to mark Caley Thistle's 3-1 Scottish Cup victory over the Parkhead club in February 2000, a result which saw John Barnes sacked as Celtic manager.

As for his own thoughts on Johnston, Gordon had this to say: 'As a young lad coming into the side playing beside someone of Johnston's stature, it was incredible. His pace, precision of pass and explosive shot was in a different league from his team-mates and opponents. He clearly should have been playing at the highest level and it was almost intimidating for me being in the same side as him. If there was one weakness to Davy's game I would say it was when he faced a one-on-one with a goalie. He invariably missed. But he was so good in the air, his pace was electrifying, and his shooting power with either foot was awesome. He was the man of the match on so many occasions but I'll never forget his performance in that Qualifying Cup final replay of 1971. He didn't get on the scoresheet but he was at the heart of everything Caley did that day and was a class act. He was a terrific team player. He was quiet but his talent commanded total respect.'

On the league front, Caley were again falling behind in their fixtures but Thistle began to close the gap on Peterhead, who crashed to three successive defeats in December, one on Christmas Day in an east coast derby against Fraserburgh.

January and February 1972 were bleak times because the country was in the grip of the miners' strike. With no fuel to run the power stations, power cuts were frequent and industry was crippled. But there was good news on the horizon for the Highlands with the announcement that oil platform construction yards were to be built at Ardersier on the Moray Firth and Nigg Bay on the Cromarty Firth. As the miners' strike came to an end and the power began to get switched back on, Thistle inaugurated their new floodlights at Kingsmills with a friendly match against Celtic which drew 6,000 fans.

But Thistle's priority was to win their first title since 1935-36. It is not without a little irony, given their manager Willie Grant's comments the previous year, that Thistle were going to need a helping hand from their Inverness neighbours. Elgin City and Thistle each had one game remaining and were joint top with 51 points. Both games were against Caley and on Saturday, 7 May 1972 there was a pitch invasion at Kingsmills when Ian Cumming scored a last-minute equaliser to cancel out a twelfth-minute goal from Johnston and keep Thistle's hopes alive.

The following Wednesday there were probably as many Thistle fans as there were Caley and Elgin supporters on the Telford Street terracing for the final showdown. Elgin were missing team captain Ally Shewan but a draw would be enough to secure a play-off. City were 2-1 up at half-time through goals from Graham and Macarthy. But the fans from Invernes were in raptures when Caley came out of the starting blocks after the change of ends and turned the game on its head. Allan, who had scored in the first half, equalised in the 49th minute and two minutes later Davy Johnston put Caley 3-2 in front. Further goals from brothers Freddie and Bobby Neild put the result beyond doubt. Another late goal from MacCarthy couldn't deny Thistle their well-deserved title glory.

Davy comes back to haunt Gers

Just six days after Caley pulled the rug from under Elgin, an Inverness Select lined up against a Glasgow Rangers team destined for European glory. Davy Johnston had collected four cup winners medals and a league championship in just two seasons since his return to the Highland League.

But some would argue that he enjoyed his finest hour in this friendly against a side which, a week later on 24 May 1972, would lift the European Cup-Winners' Cup. Several players in the Rangers party that night (Willie Mathieson, John Greig, David Smith and Willie Johnston among them) still had nightmares of the day Davy dashed their faint championship hopes on the last day of the 1967-68 season when he was with the Dons. Davy now came back to haunt Rangers one last time in this testimonial for his lifelong pal and team-mate Chic Allan, and Clach stalwarts Ally Chisholm and Ernie Latham.

No one was to know it would be the last time they were to see Chic play, for a couple of months later he died in a tragic accident falling from a hotel window in Stornoway.

Peter Corbett, who followed his father Dan into local politics and became a Highland councillor, was in that select side that lost 2-5 against Rangers. But he remembers they give the Gers one hell of a fright that evening on 17 May before 7,000 spectators at Clach's Grant Street. Nicknamed 'Rocky', Peter was a no-nonsense defender who played for all three Inverness clubs during an illustrious career. He was as honest and hard-working a player on the park as he was as a local politician off it. A real chip off the old block, like his father, who has fought doggedly for constituents in one of the most deprived areas of the city.

'Davy had put two past Peter McCloy before half-time,' recalled Peter. 'They were typical Johnston scorchers and McCloy didn't have a ghoster. We were 2-1 up at half-time, so Willie Waddell the Rangers manager beefed up his side in the second half. John Greig, their captain, came on and Rangers came through to win, but they got a real scare just days before one of their most important games in their lives. Davy had been used to playing against players at that level and he proved that night he could still do it three years later. We went for a dinner at the Haughdale Hotel after the match and Waddell was asked what price he would give for Davy. He asked Davy how old he was and I always remember Davy's reply: "Thirty Mr Waddell." [actually, Davy was 29]. A lot of players even in these days would refer to their managers by their first names but Davy was a perfect gentleman and always gave them their full title. Willie Waddell just said "a couple of years ago" and there was a pause as he raised his eyebrows. You could see by the look on his face he would have snapped him up in a second if he was looking for a striker. I was involved in Highland League football for 40 years as a player and a manager and he was unquestionably the best I have ever seen.'

Bill McAllister, one of the most knowledgeable writers on the Highland League scene, captured this classic Johnston performance in the *P&J*. 'If the Russians could recruit former Aberdeen centre-forward Dave Johnston to play for Moscow Dynamo in the European Cup-Winners' Cup final in Barcelona, the Rangers manager Willie Waddell would have a major headache this morning,' he wrote. McAllister went on to describe how Johnston gave the Ibrox defence a real runaround. Johnston's goals he said were brilliant, each fit enough to win a European trophy on their own.

The first came after an own-goal by Robbie Giles put Gers in front. In the 33rd minute Johnston set the ground and the fans alight when he ran on to a Bobby McLean pass and drilled the ball past McCloy from fifteen yards. The select had their tails up and two minutes from the interval Davy showed his blistering turn of speed when he gathered a great through pass and dispatched another gem past the helpless McCloy as the Rangers defenders continued to play catch-up.

McAllister described how Rangers' Player of the Year Dave Smith was obviously given the task of marking Johnston at half-time because Waddell was acutely aware the striking ace could do them further damage in the second half – and that was the last thing he wanted just one week before their date with destiny in Spain.

Johnston continued to cause problems after half-time but Waddell brought on captain John Greig, who was recovering from injury, to steady his ship and the Ibrox side turned the game around. Greig in fact came on for another Caley star of the future, Andy Penman. Rangers' equalising goal, though, was the subject of much debate. Select defender Bobby Noble rose in the box to grab the ball with both hands, thinking offside had been given. But the referee pointed to the spot and Tommy McLean converted. Further goals from Willie Mathieson, Willie Johnston and

McLean again, gave Gers the morale-boosting victory they were needing – but there was no doubt they got a fright that night and nearly finished on the receiving end of another hiding by Johnston.

The *P&J* columnist cited Johnston as the star player of the evening and Robbie Giles and Corbett as the other top performers for the select, with Willie Mathieson, Dave Smith and Tommy McLean taking the plaudits for Rangers. But McAllister's most telling comment of the whole spectacle was about Davy: 'His performance showed just how much the Dons lost when he walked out of First Division football three years ago because he was homesick.'

Rangers were none the worse from their fright in the Highlands and a week later they won the Cup-Winners' Cup, beating Moscow Dynamo 3-2 in Spain. For the record, the testimonial teams were:

Inverness select: Windsor (Clach); Corbett (Clach), Noble (Caley); Dingwall (Clach), Giles (Clach), Lazenby (Thistle); Johnston (Caley), Allan (Caley), Lynas (Caley), Park (Caley), Maclean (Thistle). Sub: Neilson for Park.

Rangers: McCloy; Jardine, Mathieson; Parlane, D Johnstone, Smith, McLean, Penman (Greig), Stein, MacDonald, W Johnston.

Referee: P E Bennett, Inverness.

For the record, nine of Rangers' starting eleven at Grant Street also started in Barcelona. The exceptions were Parlane, replaced by Greig in Spain, and Penman, replaced by Alfie Conn.

Incidentally, this testimonial was a re-run of another between an Inverness Select and Rangers which took place twenty years earlier. Willie Waddell was in the Rangers team that day. Goals from Ginger Mackenzie and Andy Mitchell had the select 2-1 up. but Rangers rallied to win 4-2. Even earlier, in 1948, Rangers came north to face Caley at Grant Street in a benefit for ex-Ranger Bobby Bolt – the attendance was a staggering 14,000. Rangers won 5-3.

Chic Allan's death stuns North football

It was just another day at the office for the eager cub reporter Gordon Fyfe when he arrived at work at the *Courier* office in Bank Lane on Thursday, 27 July 1972. But it turned to one of horror when the news filtered through that Chic Allan had been killed in an accident that morning. Chic had fallen from a hotel window in Stornoway where he had staying on a business trip. His body was discovered at 6am by a hotel porter on a concrete path below his room. Investigations concluded that Chic had washed his socks and put them out on a window sill to dry. But he plunged to his death when a sock fell and he tried to retrieve it.

This event, according to Davy's widow and many who knew him well, including Gordon, had a devastating impact on Davy Johnston who seemed to lose his appetite for the game after the death of his closest pal. Gordon was one of the younger players at Caley who Chic had taken under his wing, and he too felt deeply the loss of a greatly respected gentleman and team-mate:

'In those days you didn't have Radio Highland or Moray Firth Radio to listen to for the headline news. It was a press day for the *Courier* and we always did a final check to see if there were any late stories we needed to cover before going to press. Chic's death stunned not just everyone at Caley but north football generally. He was such a well-liked guy. He took me under his wing at Caley and I often went swimming with him at the pool at Nairn. Myself and Davy went to games and training in Chic's car. Davy and Chic had been inseparable from their school days and Davy took it very hard.'

Chic was a sales representative with MacRae & Dick, whose garage was in Strothers Lane, right in the heart of Inverness. My brother Sandford later told me Chic would often give him a lift in his company Austin Maxi if he saw him standing waiting for a bus at Nairn to travel to Inverness College. He was a frequent visitor to Stornoway on business and regularly stayed at the County Hotel, where the accident happened. Investigations later confirmed there were no suspicious circumstances to the death. Chic had been married only two years and north football mourned the loss of one its finest ambassadors.

After joining Nairn at the age of seventeen, Chic picked up two North Cup medals before his move to Caley in August 1965. As well as a great goalscorer himself, his bustling style and strong physique created many openings for others. In his seven seasons with Caley, Chic Allan won five Scottish Qualifying Cup medals, a Highland League championship medal in 1970-71, two Highland League Cup medals, and scored 290 goals.

An obituary penned in the *Inverness Courier* had this to say about Chic: 'It was not, however, the number of goals which he scored, or the number of medals he won, which gained for Chic Allan the respect and regard which he enjoyed in football circles. He was always a clean, sporting player, and one who always took a personal interest in young players and tried to help them.'

Chic Allan's funeral was held in Nairn at the church I have attended since I was a child. The Congregational Church, now the United

Reformed Church, is quite a landmark for travellers passing through Nairn because of the glazed hall beside the A96 trunk road through the town. I went to the funeral myself but couldn't get in the doors. I have recollections of the service being relayed to mourners outside by speakers. The church sanctuary holds a congregation of about 300. Over 1,000 people turned up to pay their own tribute to Chic, so most of the mourners were outside listening to the words of comfort provided by the minister, the Rev Alex Jackson, who explained the circumstances of the tragedy. The funeral cortege made its way to Auldearn Churchyard where scores of wreaths from Chic's friends lay.

Not that Chic would ever be forgotten, but a trophy in his memory is still competed for by teams in the North Caledonian League. Chic's brother Geordie was his biggest fan, who followed his career and Davy's career both at Nairn and Caley. Sadly, Geordie is no longer with us either. But many who knew him remember fondly his great sense of humour and how he loved regaling tales of the triumphs of his brother and Davy over a dram in his local – the Lion Hotel. Very much a part of village life in Auldearn, the pub sadly closed its doors a few years ago. Now it seems only a matter of time before developers move in and demolish it, no doubt to be replaced by housing.

The impact on Davy Johnston of Chic's death perhaps can best be gauged from statistics provided by Caley fan Ian Davidson. His meticulous record-keeping reveals that Davy scored only 33 goals in the three seasons he remained with Caley following the tragedy. In the 1972-73 season, the one after Chic died, Dave played only eighteen games, scoring eleven goals. It was a barren year, for the club found themselves playing second fiddle to a great Inverness Thistle side. Caley finished in seventh place with 30 points from 30 games.

Thistle beat Fraserburgh 5-4 in the Highland League Cup at Elgin in September, and in November the Scottish Qualifying Cup (North) was adorned with their red and black ribbons. After a 2-0 win at Kingsmills, Thistle lost the second leg 3-4 to Ross County at Victoria Park to win the trophy 5-4 on aggregate. Thistle had been unbeaten until then, but their cup exploits inevitably saw them fall behind in their league fixtures. Caley, in fact, were in contention for the title and were lying third in the table on Hogmanay 1972. But January defeats by Buckie and Keith saw their challenge go into terminal decline.

For Thistle, though, who had only lost one home game in the 1972 calendar year – to Caley in the Scottish Cup in January – they began putting pressure on the other front runners in the title race, Ross County and Huntly. A 4-2 win at Telford Street on Boxing Day saw them go top and another 4-3 derby win against Clach on Hogmanay put them joint top of the table with Huntly on 28 points, but Thistle had four games in hand. They lost their unbeaten league record for the season when they went down 4-6 at Forres in the last week in January, and the following week were knocked out of the Scottish Cup, 0-3 at Ayr before 6,318 fans (gate receipts were £1,423).

The jitters had set in, and in the last game of the season Thistle needed a draw to clinch the title against Ross County at Victoria Park. A win for the Dingwall side would earn them a play-off place. Two goals just before half-time by Alan Gray and Jim Savage put County in a commanding position. Brian D'Arcy gave Thistle a fighting chance when he turned the ball home in the 53rd minute. Ross County withstood the inevitable onslaught, winning 2-1 to set up an all-or-nothing play-off for the first time in fifteen seasons.

Thistle retained the title when they reversed the 2-1 scoreline in another thriller before a crowd on 3,182 at Telford Street on Monday, 7 May. Savage put Ross County ahead in 32 minutes but when Ian Stephen equalised for Thistle in 55 minutes they soon had their opponents on the ropes. It came as no surprise when Charlie Duncan grabbed the winner in 67 minutes to the delight of the ecstatic Thistle fans.

Thistle: Reilly, R Fraser, D'Arcy, Duthie, Bremner, McBey, T Fraser, Stephen, MacLaren, Duncan, Black.

Ross County: Bain Gordon, Brett, Seaton, Sokolowski, Lornie, Savage, Fleming, Gray, Urquhart, Hosie (Clark).

Although Davy played more games in his last two seasons with Caley, his scoring rate continue to drop alarmingly.

Caley opened their social club in Greig Street at the start of 1973-74, with chairman Dave Birrell pulling the first pint. With 500 members, there were hopes the income it would generate would turn around the fortunes of the team, but the only high point was a North of Scotland Cup win over Clach, Davy's last medal with the club. Brankin scored the winner in 78 minutes and Alan Presslie, the Caley captain who lost in four previous north finals, was carried shoulder high by his team-mates to collect the trophy. Caley finished the season in a disappointing eighth place, while Thistle, champions the previous two seasons, finished second, five points behind Elgin City.

Significantly, in fourth place were Nairn County, who were making significant strides under new manager Innes Macdonald. They finished fifth, eight points behind Elgin. Davy Johnston scored twelve goals in 24 games in this, his penultimate year in the blue of Caley: four of those, though, came in the North Cup run.

His last season was another disappointing one for a Caley club with such big ambitions. There were no trophies but they climbed to a respectable fourth place in the table as another Inverness club, Clach, pipped Keith for the title. Caley also retained the North of Scotland Cup with a 3-0 win over Elgin, but Davy missed out on the final through injury, although two of his goals helped get them there.

At the end of the 1974-75 season Davy took his leave from Telford Street, having scored ten goals in 29 appearances. It was another controversial flashpoint in his career because he was still under contract and the Telford Street club would not release him – not, at least, until later that year when an unknown benefactor came up with the cash so he could return to the club where it had all started – Nairn County. It was the third time Davy had broken his contract with a football club. Nevertheless, Caley fans of that era today still talk in awe of Johnston, but also of that great partnership with his lifelong pal Chic, which so sadly ended three years previously.

There may be some readers of this book who would question how good Johnston really was, given the fact his senior career never reached the heights of other Highland League stars such as Colin Hendry (Blackburn), Des Bremner (Aston Villa), Kevin Macdonald (Liverpool), Steve Paterson (Manchester United) and Duncan Shearer (Aberdeen). But people who were part of the Caley set-up throughout Johnston's Telford Street career are in no doubt he was the finest player ever to come out of the Highlands.

Hamish Munro, the Caley trainer during that era, spoke to me before his sudden and unexpected death as I carried out my research for this book. He had this to say: 'Yes, Davy was an enigma. You never really knew what he was thinking about off the park and the only person who ever really got close to Davy was Chic. They had an incredible bond, having played together from a very early age. Davy was quiet and Chic was much more outgoing but they were both fine lads. In fact, I think probably the biggest mistake the south clubs made when they came after Davy Johnston's signature was not offering Chic a deal as well. When Davy joined Hearts, then Aberdeen, he never really settled. I am certain that would never have happened had they taken Chic as well.

'Chic wasn't as good as Davy but he was a skilful player and a stronger personality and could easily have held his own at the top level. From their early years at Nairn they were obviously a deadly pairing. Chic was a great influence on Davy and was someone he confided in. Davy's only failing was his lack of passion. He wasn't boastful or confident and these were traits which earned him respect. He was the most unassuming individual you could wish to meet. Off the pitch he was good company but he was a very private person. After a game he would just leave and say he had a gig with his band. When I heard we were getting him from Aberdeen I couldn't believe it. It was a fantastic deal for us. He was a privilege to watch and I was so proud to have known him.'

Hamish, who was the coach of that Inverness Select which gave Rangers such a fright in that testimonial game prior to Rangers' date with destiny, said it often annoyed him when people questioned Johnston's status in the game:

'You have to remember these Rangers players were playing for their cup final places and anyone who saw Johnston that night will tell you he was head and shoulders above anyone on that park. Duncan Shearer was capped several times for Scotland and he was a good player – but Davy was different class. Willie Grant was a fantastic Highland League player but he needed people around him to make things happen. Davy could make things happen himself with that tremendous burst of speed and shooting power. If I rated Davy at 98 per cent from being the complete footballer, Willie was at 70 per cent and that's not being disrespectful to Willie who was an awesome goalgrabber. When he put on a strip, Davy grew a foot taller and when he got the ball to his feet he knew exactly what he wanted to do with it. He was so good on the park he didn't need to talk himself up off it, and of course he never did. I worked as a brickie on building sites with Davy and at lunch time I would have a kickabout with the younger lads. Davy was quite happy to sit around playing a game of cards. They would ask how good Davy really was and I would just shake my head and say "you'll never know". He wasn't one for showing off and it wasn't just as a footballer that I admired Davy. I admired him as a person – he was a thoroughly nice individual.'

Bobby Neild, who played for Caley from 1966 until 1975, echoed Munro's sentiments: 'He was the most unassuming individual you could meet and the perfect role model for some of the younger players we had at the club, like Billy Urquhart, who went on to play for Rangers. Davy was the kind of player you would find everywhere on the pitch. That's the mark of a class player, when they are always available to take a pass. Chic and Davy were a tremendous double act.'

Bobby Neild, in fact, revealed that at the age of eighteen he nearly signed for Nairn to replace Davy when he joined Aberdeen: 'I had just completed two seasons at Thistle and was scoring around fifteen goals a season. I was interviewed by Tom Walls, the Nairn chairman, who wanted me to fill Davy's shoes. It was much easier for me to sign for Caley where my brother Freddie was already playing and I could travel with him from our home in Kingussie. Davy was just an outstanding athlete who could do everything at top speed, and had he been more ambitious he could have played at the very highest level. In our Scottish ties we played against many Scottish internationalists and Davy was head and shoulders above them. But he was so quiet. Then, when he got that ball at his feet, anything could happen. In truth, players respected Davy as much for the kind of person he was as the type of footballer he was.'

Boyhood pal Alan Watson recalled a story told to him after the select match by (the late) John 'Jake' Main, who was an avid follower of Davy's career: 'After the first goal went in, big John told me he shouted towards the Rangers keeper Peter McCloy [affectionately known as the Girvan Lighthouse]: "Aye Peter you never saw that one and there's more to come." This prophecy, of course, was not misplaced. Johnston had a second goal by half-time and afterwards McCloy shook Davy's hand and told him these were two of the best goals that went past him all season.

Back to Nairn – The Title at Last

Davy's playing career came full circle when Innes Macdonald made his move in October 1975 and brought him back to Station Park. Davy had walked out on Caley in April of that year, and announced he was quitting the game. The club had suspended him and stopped his wages but Nairn came in, and after twice having bids rejected, they were successful with a third offer, Caley obviously taking the view that it was better to offload Johnston. Innes describes later in this chapter his delight in signing a player he says without question was the most gifted player he had ever seen in the Highland League. It was an emotional homecoming for both the player and his army of fans.

Johnston's departure from Caley, like that from Aberdeen and, much earlier, from Hearts, was cloaked in controversy. Countless people I have spoken to have said Davy couldn't handle confrontation and his way of dealing with problems was to walk away. After Chic's death he had become unsettled at Telford Street. He just wanted out and he followed the same path he had taken at Pittodrie and Tynecastle.

His fans at Nairn were hoping a return to Station Park would reignite his career. Even approaching his 33rd birthday, he was very fit and with a football brain that would have stood him in good stead to continue playing for years to come. But he was to play only twelve league games in a season when Nairn's long wait for that elusive championship flag would at last come to an end. We were only to see occasional glimpses of the

Davy Johnston we all knew of old and loved. That he contributed to the championship success, however, there is no doubt. Particularly memorable were the two goals he scored – one against his former club Caley, and the other against Peterhead, his last in Nairn County's colours, which I will come to later.

The season was well under way before an agreement was struck between Caley and Nairn to release the player from his Telford Street contract. Funds had been made available to Nairn by an anonymous fan to broker the deal. It is fortuitous, to say the least, that Davy played in this league-winning side because it gives me the opportunity in this book to finish the story of the club's quest for the title after the championship disappointments of 1964 and 1965. As a young reporter at the *Nairnshire Telegraph,* to be reporting football on Saturdays, after a week of the parish pump journalism which is part and parcel of every local paper, was a bit of a busman's holiday. There is no question, however, that had it not been for a stroke of good fortune this chapter in the club's history would never have been written.

I say good fortune because without Innes Macdonald as manager Nairn would not have won the league. The mastermind behind many Elgin City championships in the late 1960s, he was invited to join Nairn at a time in which he was disenchanted with the boardroom politics at Borough Briggs. Nairn County committee member Martin Robertson happened to be a teaching colleague of Innes, who was deputy Rector at Elgin Academy, and Martin was aware he was unhappy with Elgin. Nairn had finished second bottom of the league in 1972-73 after Eric Geddes became terminally ill, and Nairn were on the look-out for someone to run the team. Martin sounded out Innes on behalf of the Nairn committee. On receiving assurances from Nairn that he would have total autonomy on team affairs, Innes took up the offer. With trainer George Welsh, Macdonald breezed into Station Park and pledged it would take him two years to build a side capable of challenging for the championship.

Macdonald was true to his word. Nairn made steady progress and finished fifth in 1973-74 and sixth in 1974-75. But the following season they made it to the play-off with Fraserburgh and won the championship on a night of high drama at neutral Borough Briggs. The summer of 1975 saw the departure of seventeen-year-old Steve 'Pele' Paterson, who joined Tommy Docherty at Manchester United. But Macdonald had always said if he was going to win the title his top priority was to have a defence that stopped leaking goals.

In July of that year Macdonald made his most significant signing. He heard of a young centre-half who had made 30 first-team appearances

for St Johnstone and had lost his place with the Perth side after a carti-
lage operation. The Nairn manager moved to sign 22-year-old Dave
Cochrane. It was a time when jobs were plentiful in the north, with the
oil yard at Ardersier always looking for men, and the big gangling stopper proved to be the final piece of the jigsaw needed to transform the
team from nearly men into winners.

Cochrane was as loud and abrasive off the park as he was on it. But
he was a natural leader and the bond between him and his manager provided the right chemistry to give Nairn that extra cutting edge. When
questions were later going to be asked by top sides like Elgin, Caley and
Ross County that season of Nairn's title credentials, the team Macdonald
shrewdly put together on a shoestring budget answered emphatically by
battering opponents into submission.

Nairn suffered their first league defeat – a 1-4 reverse at Peterhead –
on the last Saturday of September, when news of Johnston's imminent
arrival began to surface. But by then Nairn had already underlined their
championship aspirations. Victories over Ross County, league champions
Clach, and a Keith side who had finished runners-up the previous season
served notice that the Wee County would be knocking on the door.

Johnston's signing, however, was not without complications. After
terms were agreed with Caley, Nairn posted Davy's registration papers on
Wednesday, 1 October 1975 to SFA headquarters at Park Gardens in
Glasgow in the belief they would arrive in time for him to make his debut
in the Qualifying Cup at Station Park three days later. Macdonald was
angry on the Saturday to learn that the registration had not gone through
because the SFA claimed not to have received the papers.

Nairn had been averaging gates of 350 to 400 per game, but 700
turned out on Saturday, 4 October for that cup-tie in anticipation of
Johnston's return. They were doubly disappointed, because not only was
Davy not eligible to play but Keith dumped them out of the cup with an
emphatic 4-0 victory.

Not prepared to let the matter rest, Nairn investigated the debacle and
proved the SFA was at fault. Jim Sutherland, a Nairn committee member,
worked with the Harbour Street Post Office and he later produced a
receipt which showed that the papers arrived at the SFA headquarters on
Thursday, 2 October. Nairn wrote to the SFA, taking them to task over
the whole affair, only to receive an abrupt reply from SFA Secretary
Willie Allan with not even a hint of an apology.

Not even Johnston's appearance the following week could stop the
rot, when Nairn lost 1-2 at home to Lossie. But they were soon back on
track with a 3-1 win over Caley at Telford Street. As well as maintaining

their challenging position in the championship race, Nairn were narrowly beaten 2-3 after extra-time in the final of the Inverness Cup by Thistle.

An arm infection had kept Davy out of the side for several games. But
he was in top form when he returned in a 4-1 drubbing of Huntly early
in December. It was a game he orchestrated from start to finish, spraying
telling passes all over the park and he laid on three of Nairn's goals.
Home and away wins against Forres over the festive season saw Nairn sitting proudly on top of the league at New Year.

Caley were Nairn's first foots of 1976 on 10 January, and the Blues
still had title aspirations of their own. It was a game which will never be
forgotten by those County fans in the stand and on the terracings that day
as Davy scored his first goal since his return in what turned out to be a
6-1 annihilation.

I remember clearly how the crowd in the old wooden stand rose to
their feet as one and gave Johnston a standing ovation when his goal went
in. Even Innes, not one for making grand gestures, and George Welsh got
out of the dugout and stood shoulder to shoulder on the touchline and
warmly applauded the returning hero's goal. It's one of these moments
you want to put in a bottle. I was able to do so and wistfully release the
cork over the passing years to savour that space in time. I am sure thousands of fans who saw Davy perform will remember as they read this –
a special moment in their own mind's eye – a moment when Davy used
his electrifying pace to destroy a defence, picked out a pass that seemed
impossible, or simply left a goalkeeper asking 'how did that get there?',
after another shot flew into the net like a rocket.

Nairn lad Ray Mackintosh had in fact put Caley ahead that day after
just 60 seconds, but Johnston laid on the equaliser for another giant in
that Nairn side, Robin Mitchell, to score on 32 minutes from a free-kick.
That signalled the start of a goal-feast. Donald Robertson and Sammy
Forsyth added two more before half-time and if Caley harboured any
hopes of a revival they were laid to rest by Johnston himself with that
memorable goal in the 47th minute. Davy started the move with a timely pass out to Norman Macdonald, and the galloping policeman stretched
the Caley defence with a powerful run before cutting the ball back for
Davy to send a cracking drive from close range into the net.

Macdonald and the industrious Alec Gordon added further goals to
complete a great afternoon's work for Nairn. But in my match report for
the *Nairnshire Telegraph* that day I had a pop at the stay-away fans – the
crowd was just 400 – a team with title aspirations surely deserved better.
The following month it was Ross County who were on the receiving end
of another Nairn thrashing. Winger Billy Mitchell, who Macdonald

signed from Aberdeen junior side Rosslyn Sport, scored a hat-trick in another crushing 5-1 win.

In their first five games of 1976, Nairn had scored twenty goals and conceded six – interesting statistics when you compare that with their first four games of the 1966-67 season, when they scored twenty but conceded 24 – adding further credence to Macdonald's theory that he needed a solid back line if he was going to win the title.

Johnston's 279th and final goal in a Nairn County shirt was scored in the league against Peterhead on 28 February 1976, and what an important goal it was. The Blue Toon side, with players of the calibre Ray O'Hara and Colin Grant, were strong contenders for the championship them-selves. They ended the season on 43 points, the same as Keith, just one behind Nairn and Fraserburgh.

The significance of this 3-1 victory perhaps went unnoticed because many Nairn fans remember the heavy defeats they inflicted that season on Caley, Ross County and later in the year on Elgin. Robin Mitchell had given Nairn the lead when he headed home a Johnston cross after six minutes, but Peterhead replied with an equaliser from Noble. It wasn't a comfortable afternoon, but Johnston restored Nairn's lead and Peter Robertson's third goal sealed the victory. Johnston was substituted late in the game but his next appearance on 6 March 1976 at Kynoch Park, when Nairn went down 1-2 to Keith, was to be his last.

It was a game where Nairn squandered many chances. They had taken the lead but Keith equalised. Nairn paid the price eight minutes from time when Sammy Forsyth, a stalwart in the defence of that title-winning side, put through his own goal to give Keith two vital points.

A trialist, Joe Flynn, appeared in Nairn's line-up the following week. Flynn, from Ayrshire juniors Hurlford United, scored two goals in a 4-2 win against Brora at Nairn but he declined a signing offer.

By now the season was reaching the home straight and another test awaited Nairn at Borough Briggs. Nairn fans had the scent of the title in their nostrils and travelled in large numbers. I remember it was my moth-er's birthday, 20 March, so I hoped that was a good omen. My father did-n't give much for Nairn's chances. He had never really forgiven Nairn for selling Johnston a decade before when City were almost unstoppable, capturing eight titles between 1960 and 1970. Imagine my delight when I rang him at half-time from a coin box in the ground to tell him Nairn were leading 4-0. In fact the margin of victory seemed even greater than the final scoreline of 5-1 suggests.

Nairn were rampant and the game was all but over as a contest after just fourteen minutes. Billy Mitchell, Norman Macdonald and Peter

Robertson were on target as Nairn surged into a 3-0 lead, leaving Elgin shell-shocked. Norman Macdonald snatched his second before half-time and Peter Robertson completed the rout on the hour, Elgin's consolation coming late in the game from Davy's former Aberdeen team-mate Jimmy Wilson. Winger Stan Brown recalls the Nairn players were angry with themselves at having allowed Elgin even that solitary goal: 'It should never have counted because our goalkeeper Richard Konczak was clattered going for the ball by their forwards,' said Stan. 'We should have scored a lot more that day and we were just angry with ourselves at conceding that one goal.'

The league table on the Monday showed Fraserburgh top with 44 points from 30 games and Nairn second, two points behind but with two games remaining. Ominously, Keith had 36 points from just 24 games.

Nairn's final matches were away, against Huntly and Rothes. Three points would put them ahead of Fraserburgh but Keith were still in the equation with their games in hand. At Christie Park an early Norman Macdonald goal was cancelled out by Donald of Huntly. Nairn's forwards squandered plenty of opportunities to get the victory they so desperately needed but they had to settle for a draw.

That result put them within touching distance of Fraserburgh. Their last game of the season the following week in a Mackessack Park mud bath on Speyside was another afternoon of frustration as they failed to find the net in a no-scoring draw on 10 April. 'We did everything but score that day,' recalled Brown. 'We hit the bar and the post but the ball just wouldn't go in. There was one occasion when the ball dropped to Donald Robertson right in front of goal. He stuck out his knee and it went over the bar from one yard. Had he let it drop it would have stuck in the mud and he could have walked it over the line.'

Nevertheless the result was enough to put them level on points with Fraserburgh and the possibility of a play-off. But both sides now had to play a waiting game as Keith caught up with their backlog of fixtures. I remember one fan saying to me at the time you're better with the points in the bag and Keith still had it all to do. How prophetic these words proved to be.

Keith's 3-1 win at Clach and a 1-0 victory against Elgin at Kynoch Park saw the maroons move to within one point of the leaders. So the stage was set for a dramatic finale. One win from two games would take the title to Keith. But both were tough fixtures – away to Peterhead and away to Elgin. One Nairn player, who had virtually been ever present that season, Brian Derby, thought it was all over and he left the area to go and work in the Channel Islands. With Fraserburgh and Nairn fans following every kick of the ball, Peterhead did their Buchan neighbours a big favour by dumping Keith 2-0 at Recreation Park. Keith then suffered a crushing midweek 1-2 defeat against Elgin at Borough Briggs to put paid to their challenge. Keith finished third.

Brown recalls nearly the entire Nairn squad were watching from the terracing and a delighted Macdonald ran onto the field at the final whistle to congratulate the Elgin players. I confess I didn't think Keith would slip up and could not bear to go. What joy the following morning when I picked up the *P&J* to check the result – Nairn's title dream was still alive.

So there was everything to play for. Nairn were looking for their first ever championship and Fraserburgh hadn't won the league since 1954-55. Nairn tried in vain to trace Brian Derby but he was to miss out on the biggest game of his career, the championship decider with the Broch. Another hero of the season, and they were all heroes to a man, was super Norman Macdonald. Like his striking partner Alex Gordon, finesse wasn't his strongest point. But I remember Innes saying to me in one interview during the course of that season that if there was one player he would want on a one-on-one with the keeper and expect to score it was the big bobby. Unfortunately, Norman was on a course with the police and couldn't be released for that unforgettable night in Elgin.

The fishing fleet at the Broch stayed in port so the fishermen could add their voice to the big support that travelled from the Buchan port. Nairn fans, too, turned out in large numbers and as kick-off approached the nerves of the players were jangling when the referee delayed the kick-off as hundreds of fans were still at the turnstiles.

If ever there was a rags to riches story, this was it. For just three seasons earlier, Nairn had avoided the wooden spoon, finishing second bottom of the league, one point ahead of Deveronvale.

Innes Macdonald sprung a major surprise when he fielded Tommy Wilson from Middlefield Wasps of Aberdeen on the wing. Nairn players met him for the first time in the dressing room minutes before the kick-off. What a night to be making your debut. A measure of his contribution can be gauged by the fact it wasn't until the fifth minute of extra-time before Macdonald decided to replace him with that other Aberdeen-based winger, Billy Mitchell.

In a nervous opening before 3,367 fans, the tension was showing on both sides but it was Nairn who had the early ascendancy. Gray was beaten by a Sammy Forsyth effort but Nairn sweeper Robin Mitchell headed over at the far post. Cross-balls continued to rain into the Fraserburgh penalty area and Peter Robertson was giving the Broch defence a torrid time with his piercing runs. Konczak was a virtual spectator in the first half in the Nairn goal and the Nairn support thought they had made the breakthrough in the 25th minute when Alex Gordon bundled the ball into the net. But the whistle had gone for a foul on the keeper.

Fraserburgh appeared stage-struck as Nairn continued to launch sortie after sortie and it came as no surprise when Nairn finally made the breakthrough a minute from half-time. Robertson headed the ball down to Stan Brown, who had been the architect of many a Nairn goal that season with that sweet left foot of his. From his cross on the edge of the box Gordon had to be at full stretch to send a rising header under the bar at the far post. Given their percentage of possession and chances created in the first half, confidence was high among the Nairn support that they would finish the job in the second half.

But Fraserbrugh had other ideas and they came storming back into the game with an equaliser in the 51st minute. Konczak punched out a long-range free-kick from Roger, only to see the ball land at the feet of Stephen who picked his spot from twelve yards.

Nairn found themselves under the cosh for spells in the second half. But the central defensive partnership of Cochrane and Mitchell wasn't yielding an inch and Nairn came close to grabbing the winner in the closing stages when Peter Robertson shaved the post with a fine header. Then Wilson blasted over from close range.

There was one last moment of drama before the whistle for 90 minutes. Nairn's keeper Richard Konczak took a nasty kick in the face from Fraserburgh striker Newlands and underwent intensive treatment during the interval before extra-time commenced. The referee in fact delayed extra-time to allow him to be treated.

Konczak later sportingly exonerated Newlands of all blame and said it was legitimate challenge for a 50-50 ball. But he admits that kick in the teeth probably earned Nairn the title. 'It's quite simple. Had Newlands connected with the ball and not my face he would have scored,' Richard admitted. Still dazed, he resumed with a gauze mask on his face and his defence under instruction from Macdonald to protect him at all costs.

Six minutes into extra-time Nairn got the clinching goal, and again it was Stan Brown who was the provider with a telling through pass for Peter Robertson, a thorn in the Fraserburgh defence the whole night. Gray came sprinting from his line on spotting the danger, but Robertson cleverly clipped the ball beyond the advancing keeper and into the net for the most important goal in the club's history.

Doug MacIldowie hit the Fraserburgh bar and then sent another drive over the top but Nairn finished worthy 2-1 winners. The game had been won without Davy Johnston, but the championship flag would now fly at Nairn for the first time.

Nairn: Konczak, McFadden, Forsyth, R Mitchell, Cochrane, Brown, Wilson (W Mitchell), D Robertson, Gordon (Hendry), MacIldowie, P Robertson.

Fraserburgh: Gray, Sharp, Cardno, Mackenzie, Roger, Duthie, Watson (Massie) Hunter, Newlands (MacKay) Stephen, Bowie.

Referee: L J S Officer, Aberdeen.

After treatment at Dr Gray's Hospital in Elgin, where he had stitches in his mouth, Richard Konczak, boarded the team bus. The returning heroes arrived in Nairn expecting to see fans dancing in the street.

But they were in for a shock, recalled Richard. 'We went up the Brae into the High Street and couldn't believe it. We were expecting the fans to be celebrating in the streets but there was not a soul there. The High Street was empty. It was like a non-event and we were disappointed. So we headed back down to Stan Brown's dad's pub, The Brackla Canteen, in Harbour Street where we found the answer. When we opened the doors there was an almighty roar and cheering. The supporters had all headed to the Canteen and the party was already in full swing. It went on all night but I was sober throughout. My mouth was numb from the stitches and when I was given a pint it just dribbled down the side. But it was an unforgettable night.'

As the years have rolled on I have often hoped Fraserburgh could make up for their disappointment that night by winning the title. I have been a great admirer of the work of Charlie Duncan, the longest serving manager in the Highland League, who has nurtured dozens of young footballers from the Broch over nearly three decades. If anyone deserves that honour it's Charlie and, of course, the Fraserburgh committee for giving local youth its chance when so many other clubs produce the cheque book to bring success.

'Johnston was the best ever' – Macdonald

There has been some debate among Nairn County fans since Innes's side annexed Nairn's first league title about the merits of that 1975-76 team compared to the side which wore the colours the previous decade.

Was it the class of 1963-64 and 1964-65, who were agonisingly pipped at the post for the title, who were the best – or was it Macdonald's battlers who never gave up the chase and were rewarded by writing their own names in the history books that night at Borough Briggs?

It was a delight for me to be reporting these matches for the *Nairnshire Telegraph* in the championship-winning season. I often had animated discussions since with the Nairn County captain Davy Cochrane, who felt he and his team-mates hadn't been given the recognition they deserved by some for their magnificent achievement.

I was too young to fully appreciate the quality of that earlier side of the 1960s. But from speaking to fans who seldom missed a match, I think in terms of sheer class they deserved the title of the best ever Nairn team, even though the league eluded them. You just have to look at the statistics in 1963-64 (Davy's record-breaking year) – 139 goals in 46 games – they must have been very special. In 30 league games they scored 99 goals and conceded 64. The class of 1975-76 scored 75 league goals but the defence conceded only 35.

But in no way would one opinion diminish the achievements of Innes Macdonald, Cochrane and the rest of the team, from Richard Konczak in goal to Stan Brown on the left wing, when they finally lifted the championship in 1976. They gave us a roller-coaster year and were battlers to a man. Your top football managers will tell you that sometimes when teams may lack the flair and finesse of a truly great side, that can be compensated by great team spirit.

I have no doubt it was that all-for-one mentality drummed into the players by Innes Macdonald and his trainer, 'gentleman' George Welsh, which saw that Nairn side through in their finest hour. They dished out some real thumpings to the top sides that season, including Elgin, Caley and Ross County. And when they took to the field that Monday evening at Borough Briggs for the all-or-nothing match with the Broch they were there on merit and deservedly took their place as true County heroes.

Innes agrees that it was the team spirit which pulled them through in the end. He didn't go into the politics of the boardroom at Borough Briggs which influenced his move to Station Park. But Innes said there were only two clubs in the Highland League he would have gone to at that time – Nairn County and Ross County:

'These were the only two grounds you could go to and know you would be treated with utter respect. At Station Park when I was with Elgin I was always greeted with a warm handshake by the chairman, Tom Walls. It was the same at Dingwall. There was a decency about the place. They were professional and extended sportsmanship before, during, and after the match. I'm afraid at so many other grounds that was not the case. Because we were so successful we could attract players from any club and some of the abuse we were subjected to in the dug-out was worse than what was going out on the pitch.'

Innes said that from the moment he took up the offer to manage Nairn the committee gave him nothing but 100 per cent backing and honoured their pledge not to interfere with the way he ran the team. And he had no doubt it was the 'team spirit and togetherness' of his players which earned them the title: 'Nairn had been built up gradually. While we had a spine of good players, it would be foolish to claim we were a team of stars. What we lacked was a top-class player and when I heard we had a chance to sign someone of Davy Johnston's calibre we leapt at it. I knew him only too well as an opponent with Elgin and we feared him. I was just thrilled to get the chance to work with Davy and my estimation of him as a player was reinforced when I saw him close up on the training ground. He was almost the complete footballer. I had been in Highland League football since the 1950s and I cannot tell you how brilliant this man was. His speed of thought, speed on the move, quick control, the intelligent passing, his ability to get a high percentage of his shots on target from any position – he had all of these qualities and there was no one to touch him.'

Davy Johnston's role was more than a cameo appearance that season. The fact that he played twelve games for Nairn in the only championship-winning year with the club he loved, was to me and many other fans the icing on the cake. It's well over three decades since that title win and Innes admitted some surprise when I told him how many games Davy had played that year.

'Sadly on Saturdays the ability we all witnessed at training on Tuesdays and Thursdays was not as evident as I hoped it would be. He had obviously lost a little but it wasn't a physical thing. I used him as a tutor in training and he could do amazing things with the ball, but he was a pale shadow of himself on the Saturday. He tended to play out of the box and that's why he never scored so many goals. I became aware that his self-confidence had been eroded in other times. He was a sensitive man and it was something outside my ken. I tried to get him to take more responsibility. The skills he could still demonstrate were breathtaking but in time illness overtook him and he dropped out of the picture. Of course, we did see glimpses of the old Davy and that goal against Caley does stick in my mind and it's a memory I still treasure.

'For years, of course, I had Willie Grant at Elgin and he was a tremendous player and unbelievably brave in the air for a guy who was only 5ft 9in. But he [Grant] never took a ball round a player in his life. He would lay it off and go into the box waiting for the cross. Davy was good in the air. He wasn't better than Willie in the air. But Willie was not high in the ball skills like Davy and his Elgin team-mate Gerry Graham. It was a great sadness when Davy quit but his health had to come first. I just felt privileged even for a short time to work with the player I certainly regarded as the best ever player to grace the Highland League in all my years in the game.'

The St Ninian Years

It may still seem strange to some readers that a footballer who played a relatively short time at the top level in the Scottish game should be so idolised. But in my research for this book the feeling that this recognition of Johnston's career was both deserved and appropriate has never diminished. I now come to the final chapter in Davy's football career which I can talk about from a personal perspective because I witnessed it at first hand. It was through his involvement with the local junior football club, Nairn St Ninian, that I got to know Davy. We have already heard testimony to his modesty and unassuming manner.

In this chapter you will hear evidence of how he never once sought to impress the players at St Ninian with tales of his Aberdeen days or his incredible scoring achievements in the Highland League. But probably like so many of his former team-mates, managers and coaches, I still question how well I really knew the person and what made him tick. At St Ninian he was a thoroughly amiable person who gave the club total commitment and was good company socially. I regarded him as a close friend and was deeply moved when his family asked me to give the eulogy at his funeral, which was attended by representatives of Aberdeen FC and clubs throughout the Highland League – a testimony to the high regard in which he was held.

I was seconded to the committee of St Ninian Football Club during the 1975-76 season – a vintage year for football in Nairn, with County winning the Highland League and Nairn St Ninian making it a league double for the town by lifting the North Regional League (North) championship. St Ninian in fact was formed just six years earlier at a meeting I attended with my father at the Shore Inn, so the club came a long way in a short time. The achievements of both clubs were recognised by Nairn District Council, which staged a civic reception for officials and players at the Lion Hotel in Auldearn.

I worked hard raising funds, along with Jock Willox, Arthur Fuge and the Ardersier contingent of Alastair Ross and Bill Mitchell. Bill Geegan, a local ambulance driver, was our manager at the start of the season we won the league, but Bill got the opportunity to step up to the Highland

League with Lossiemouth mid-term and Hugh Cowper, a Maths teacher at Nairn Academy, took over the reins to guide the club to the title. The following season things went downhill and truth to tell I can't remember why. But we were struggling both on the field and off the field. We lost our manager and several committee members and if you don't have stability off the park it makes it doubly difficult for the players to focus on it. Financially we were having difficulty making ends meet and as a reporter in the local paper I made an impassioned appeal for new blood to help run the affairs of the club in the *Nairnshire Telegraph*.

The call was answered. Not only did we get several new volunteers for the committee: we learned that Davy had expressed an interest in becoming our manager. Having hero-worshipped him throughout his career, myself and most of the players who knew of Davy's status in the game were dumbstruck when we heard the news. Although untried as a coach, we went on the premise that his standing in the game would command automatic respect of the players. It took no persuasion, and the newly formed committee wasted no time in accepting Davy's offer.

We weren't disappointed and he took the club to a different level, winning successive league titles and significantly giving the north junior section a side that offered a serious challenge to the big Aberdeen clubs from the east section in inter-regional competitions.

Davy was working at the time at McDermott's oil fabrication facility at Whiteness Head, Ardersier, now zoned for an exclusive resort village with a 500-berth sailing marina. Many of the great platforms still operating in the North Sea, including the ill-fated Piper Alpha, were built there. But as I've said before, the industry brought many skilled men up from the central belt of Scotland. The shipbuilding and heavy manufacturing down south was on the decline, and with highly paid jobs and a beautiful environment in which to live, it was a no-brainer for many to move their families lock, stock and barrel to the Highlands.

The point should not be missed either that herein lay an added bonus for local football clubs. The yards at Ardersier and Nigg on the Cromarty Firth were to provide employment at their peak for nearly 7,000 men, and among them a rich seam of footballing nuggets who went on to make their mark in the Highland League and the local junior game – not least Davy Cochrane who skippered Nairn County and later managed St Ninian for a spell after Johnston.

Another bonus from the yard was these guys were earning top-dollar wages by local standards and they were very generous in their support of sweepstakes and all manner of lotteries to keep wee clubs like ours afloat. My two elder brothers, Alastair and Sandford, and my late father Eddie all gave up their respective trades to head for the 'gold' at the oil yard at Whiteness Head. I resisted that temptation and continued my career in journalism.

Eric Robertson, Grant Fraser, Davie Proctor, Andy Donaldson and Jim Ness were just some of the names recruited to the committee and they all knew Davy and his former Aberdeen team-mate Ally Shewan who were working at 'the yard'. They had sounded him out and it was a foregone conclusion when his offer was presented to the committee that we would accept.

At this point in his life Davy was divorced from his wife Margaret after difficulties in their marriage. But they got together again, remarried and had another son, Trevor, who has helped me in the research for this book. Margaret nursed Davy through his illness and he was surrounded by his family when he died of cancer at the age of 61 in 2004.

It is often said that good footballers don't always make good managers but, for a junior club which was on its uppers, getting someone of Davy's stature was an incredible stroke of luck. It was evident from the start of the 1977-78 season that his influence was going to transform our fortunes after the debacle the previous year.

Although I had seen Davy Johnston play often, I had never met him personally, apart from shaking hands with him briefly as a starry-eyed member of the Nairn County Supporters Club when he returned to Station Park with the Aberdeen team for a friendly match in 1966. That was was part of the deal when he signed from Nairn County, and Davy scored two goals in a 5-2 win for the Dons. Starstruck youngsters waited outside the stand for autographs after the match and I was the envy of my mates when Aberdeen star Jens Petersen handed me the tie-ups he used for his stockings.

The next time Davy and I met was at a committee meeting in the Hermitage Hotel and my recollection was he made no rash promises. One thing that struck me immediately, though, was that I was speaking to a thoroughly modest individual. This is a world of football prima donnas, they can be found in abundance – yes, at every level of the game – even in the pub leagues. People who couldn't have laced Davy's boots would have you believe they were the next answer to Pele.

In Davy Johnston you had an individual who had done his talking on the park. He certainly didn't need to talk himself up off it. All our players knew he was the real deal, and from our goalie Ian Hendry, our skipper and centre-half Raymond Sharp, through to the front line led by our centre-forward Willie Barron and Dougie Storm, he had automatic respect. It was the beginning of a very happy union for over two years.

Then Davy had a second spell with the club in the mid-1980s before retiring from the game completely.

As the players got to know Davy on the training ground, the committee – I confess myself included – got to know him at the Wee Bar at the Regal. Located in Nairn at the corner of Leopold Street and the main A96 trunk road, it is now a forlorn sight, lying empty awaiting developers to move in and demolish it as part of a much-vaunted town-centre redevelopment. Many a happy evening we spent at the Regal. The Wee Bar formed part of the local bingo hall.

Davy made it clear at the outset when he joined St Ninian that it was not his intention to be a player-manager, although such a prospect is one the committee would have relished. In fact, he did register as a player but it was clear he saw his role solely as a manager.

Not only was the Wee Bar a great place for socialising. Davy and the committee had many friends there. Robert Fairlie was the owner of the complex which had two bars and a cinema. There was a dance floor which became a roller-skating rink on Saturday mornings, but the pull of the cinemas in Inverness signalled the death knell for 'the pictures' in Nairn and towards the end of its lifetime the hall was used for bingo.

Staff and regulars knew us all and supported us financially in our endeavours to keep the club going. Harry Schonewille was the manager there and we recruited him on to the committee. So with Mr Fairlie's blessing we had the run of the place as far as fund-raising was concerned. At half-time during bingo, there was a roaring trade to be done selling lottery tickets, and after the second session of bingo we'd retire to the bar where there was no shortage of volunteers, myself included, to give a song and Davy was happy to give a tune on his mouth-organ.

On a Sunday night we would head for the Hermitage Hotel about 10pm where the owner, Edwin Moar, would take out his accordion for a sing-song to round off the evening. A proud Orcadian, Edwin was one of the finest accordionists going. In the 1960s he regularly featured in the popular Grampian TV series *Bothy Nichts* and his passing was a great loss to traditional music in the area.

Before Edwin died he encouraged me to become involved in the Nairn Ceilidh Group, which still plays to big crowds every Thursday summer evening at the British Legion Hall and has a long tradition of raising funds for deserving local causes. In the late 1970s the expansive grounds of the Hermitage were used for our summer fetes. The hotel itself was a beautiful mansion once owned by Dr John Grigor, a nineteenth century ship's surgeon who transformed Nairn into a tourist resort. The building was demolished in the 1990s to make way for a specialist care home.

But the fetes that locals will remember were fantastic events in a beautiful setting. After the usual stalls and games on the lawn in the afternoon, the festivities would be rounded off with a marquee disco in the evening. Our president by this time was a local woodcutter, Jock Willox, who I have already mentioned was one of the founder members of the club. Anyone who knew Jock regarded him as Mr St Ninian. It was Jock, who was a larger than life character, who got me roped into the committee.

Looking back I see similarities between Jock and Bob Gordon, who was the chairman of Nairn County Football Club when they won the league. They were both raconteurs who could sell snowballs to the eskimos. Jock knew how to sell tickets and a lot of that rubbed off on me. Bob, in fact, was instrumental in getting a social club built for Nairn County in the shell of the derelict Playhouse Cinema in Church Street.

He was also responsible for getting Nairn's first set of floodlights erected at Station Park. The 30-foot lighting poles were manufactured at McDermott's. Bob could be very persuasive when Nairn County was concerned and McDermott's management went about their business helping the local community quietly and without fuss. The lights are still in use today, supplementing stronger floodlights which were relocated from Caley's former Telford Street ground. That land was bought by developers and transformed into a retail park after Caley's amalgamation with Thistle to join the Scottish League, when the new club moved to a new ground beside the Kessock Bridge.

People like Bob Gordon and Jock Willox were invaluable to football clubs in that era. Fetes, coffee mornings, raffles and sponsored walks were the order of the day, unlike the more sophisticated financial management required even at Highland League level these days.

I've mentioned the support the club received from the local community, and never more so was that evident than when St Ninian later embarked on its biggest ever financial undertaking to build new changing rooms at the Showfield. What existed there before was a primitive shelter effectively constructed of partitions attached to the old stables used for horses when Indian soldiers were billeted in the field during the Second World War. Rudimentary plumbing was installed to provide showers and toilets beneath a corrugated tin roof but it was a very cramped and damp environment. The electricity was supplied by a cable running from the garage of a neighbouring house and it was not unusual to find the premises on the morning of a match had been infiltrated by vagrants or young people for drinking sessions.

On one occasion we found a Calor gas heater, which had been bought to take the chill off the place, had been used overnight as a barbecue for sausages. Then one morning myself and other committee members arrived to find the main partition had been knocked down by vandals and was effectively lying flat on what was the concrete floor of the dressing rooms. We lifted up the partition, nailed it back in place with six-inch spikes, and we set about laying out the strips for that day's match as if nothing had happened. The players arrived an hour before kick-off completely unaware that their changing facilities had been hastily rebuilt that morning.

But that incident was a catalyst. It was time for action and with the team still flying high under Davy's guidance it was an opportune period in the club's history to harness local goodwill that existed for the club. I applied for grants and the planning process that had to be gone through. One of our players, Dougie MacLean, drew up the plans, while the rest of the committee and everyone else set about serious fund-raising, largely through lottery ticket sales. Eric Robertson, one of our committee, set up a network of salesmen and women throughout the McDermott's yard, from the pipemill to the canteens, to store rooms to rolling mills. I'm told tickets were even sold by agents 200 feet up on the platforms as they were being built. For my own part, I made sure I was at the Regal bingo sessions at half-time where I could shift 200 tickets during the twenty-minute intervals. The lottery was national and tailored for Scottish Junior Football Association clubs. But after a while we launched our own lottery – the first club to do so with a top prize of £1,000.

We also had to secure a 21-year-lease of the Showfield from the owners of the ground, the Nairnshire Farming Society. They couldn't have been more accommodating and their president, Sandy Forbes, negotiated a deal which would provide the Society with an annual income but not place the football club under undue financial pressure. His help was pivotal in moving the proposals forward.

The building was to cost £25,000 and it opened in March 1983 and is still in use today. The present committee continued to soldier on, facing the same financial pressures that we faced. However, for a spell the ground had been the subject of speculation for development, and although its long-term future is uncertain, recent developments, including the construction of a boundary fence round the playing surface, suggests Saints could be playing there for some time yet.

The Scottish Junior Football Association has done itself no favours by its reconstruction of the game, leaving St Ninian at times competing in a north league with little more than six clubs. Promotion means they would go into a larger league that would involve them in much longer and costly journeys to fulfil their fixtures. One Morayshire club, Fochabers, were suspended from the league after winning the title because they realised taking the step up would bankrupt them. Fostering football at grass roots seems to take second place to the bloody-mindedness of bureaucrats in football at all levels.

I would like to think during my spell with St Ninian I always acted with integrity and honesty in the best interests of the club. But I confess to involving myself in a bit of jiggery-pockery with Jock Willox in order to extract funds from Nairn County for the signature of our star striker Willie Barron at the end of the 1977-78 season.

Innes Macdonald had been keen to get Willie on his books. But Saints were challenging for the title and in the final stages of several cups. Willie was clear he wanted to see the season out at the Showfield. Despite his twenty cigarettes a day habit, he was the fastest thing on two feet in the junior realm and he was a prolific scorer. When the season ended we heard no more from Nairn until a midweek pre-season match at Station Park in the summer of 1978 when Innes approached me and asked again about signing Willie Barron. I was aware that Willie had not registered for the following season with St Ninian. We discussed the situation with Davy Johnston and it was agreed that we would get Willie on a form immediately so we would get a fee for his transfer. The following night at training we explained our situation to Willie, who was happy to sign on the dotted line. He was a loyal player.

Our difficulty was we had to get the registration form down to SFA headquarters at Park Gardens – and quickly. It so happened that Gordon Main our treasurer was travelling south to Glasgow at the weekend to watch a Rangers game. He volunteered to take the form into Park Gardens, so by the time we were to meet the County officials after their match on the Saturday, Willie would be a signed St Ninian player – albeit his registration having taken place only a few hours earlier.

I attended Nairn's friendly match at Station Park that day with Jock, with the intention of making the short journey along to the Hermitage Hotel afterwards to complete the deal which would make our prized striker a Nairn County player. But during the course of the afternoon word reached us there had been an error in the form and the SFA would not accept Willie's registration. I went into panic mode and was firmly told by Jock to shut up and plead ignorance. We went up to the Hermitage and did the deal. Among those present was Alex Y Cameron, the local burgh surveyor (known to his friends as AY), who was the secretary of Nairn County. I felt a bit guilty because I knew Alex well. He was an honest broker, loved his football and the town and I had got to know him well through my work with the local newspaper. We accepted a cheque for £200 from Nairn County for Willie's signature to join the Highland League.

The County officials left happily, having completed the transaction, and I think Jock's words to me were 'make sure that cheque goes into the bank first bloody thing on Monday morning'. The cheque was banked and everyone from our end sang dumb. But the following Friday I went into the Seaforth Club, which was my favourite haunt after work at the end of a busy week. Bob Gordon was the manager of the club and when he saw me come into the bar he beckoned me over to his table, where he was enjoying a dram with AY and Bill Smith, a former County player himself, who ran a local joinery businesses, and Rodwill Clyne. Bob had a quiet word in my ear to the effect that they had found out Willie Barron was not a registered St Ninian player after all.

I continued to play the dumb laddie and said I had witnessed the form being signed. Truth be told I had raised questions about how the form had been completed. I raised the matter at the time but I never pushed the issue and the form was given to Gordon to take to Park Gardens. No more was said about the whole affair and, to be fair to County, they never asked for the fee to be repaid. Legally they had us over a barrel. But Willie would not have wanted to join them without St Ninian getting some form of compensation, such was his loyalty to the club, and I have a clear conscience over the whole matter.

Things didn't work out for Willie Barron at Station Park and the following season he was back doing what he enjoyed most – scoring goals for Saints. We certainly weren't complaining. It was great to have him back.

His son, also Willie, who shared his father's great burst of speed, went on to become a regular for Nairn County and to captain the club. He recently quit football and like his dad is a formidable golfer. Playing off a handicap of plus one, he became the Nairn County Champion in 2010.

Over the next couple of seasons a few of our players departed to Nairn and Forres, and these clubs were nothing less than honourable, ensuring we were recompensed in some way. They knew they could sign these players for nothing when their registration expired at the end of each season because they weren't being paid by St Ninian. But they recognised the value of junior teams in bringing players along to a level where they are ready for the step up to Highland League. The same, however, could not be said for Inverness Caley, who signed one of our most talented midfield players, Andy Murray. We received no payment for his services and although, strictly speaking, Caley were within their rights, it left a bitter taste. A few months into his Caley career Andy broke his leg.

We were heart-sorry for the lad, whose Caley career seemed to end before it even started.

There were many characters around the club at the time, not least Willie Barron's dad, Tommy. A local plumber, he was aptly nicknamed ballcock. Often he travelled to away games on the team bus accompanied by Michael Ross, our club mascot. Mike had Down's Syndrome but his dad Colin ensured he lived life to the full and he was loved by everyone associated with St Ninian. He had a great sense of fun and on one occasion on a bus trip coming back from a game he was getting a bit of ribbing from the boys and he shocked everyone by pulling down his trousers and wiggling his bottom at the players – fortunately he still had his long johns on. Tragically, Mike died after being knocked down by a car as he got off a bus on the A96 trunk opposite his home in Boathpark. Players and officials of St Ninian turned out *en masse* to pay their own tribute to Mike at his funeral.

A popular member of Davy Johnston's backroom team at the Showfield was Ali Ross. Ali was the youngest brother of Dave Ross, who played for Nairn County. Ali was a very talented footballer with a bright future until a trampolining accident at school caused a neck injury which brought the early onset of arthritis and other health problems. Ali could run rings round the bigger lads at football and I am certain he would have made his mark in the game. But despite his debilitating condition he played at Welfare League level, then joined us on the committee at St Ninian. He was Davy's physio for several years with Saints and he was liked and respected for his knowledge of the game by all the players and committee.

Then one day we heard the news he had died of a heart attack in an ambulance on the way to Raigmore Hospital. He was still in his twenties. It was a great shock to the community and of course to his elderly parents, who lived at the corner of William Street and Whitelaw Crescent, where there was always a warm welcome for myself, and Ali's pals from Queenspark where we grew up together.

Many an evening we spent watching David Coleman's *A Question of Sport*, and more often than not it was Ali, who was fiercely competitive, who would emerge triumphant. But he will never be forgotten in Nairn. A handsome trophy was donated to the local Welfare League and it is still competed for annually.

As well as Dave, Ali had three more brothers, Robert, who made the army his career, and Arthur and Ronald. Arthur, or 'Pop' as he was to everyone, worked at the oil yard and Ronald was a mechanic by trade. I still have vivid memories on those warm summer nights at the Riverside pitch when there was a match on. Ronald would appear from his work at Macrae & Dicks garage in his tackety boots and boiler suit. He thought nothing of joining in a kickabout behind the goals – tackety boots and all. Players were well advised to keep clear when they saw him coming.

My involvement with St Ninian in fact brought about a meeting with with one of Aberdeen's Gothenburg greats, Neil Simpson. In fact I even got to play in the same team as him. Neil's playing career had ended and he was by this time a qualified SFA coach. He was looking for facilities to hold coaching sessions with the local schools and I arranged for him to use the Showfield. A friendly match had also been arranged between the coaches and a Nairn County/St Ninian select and I was invited to play in the coaches' side.

At half-time I told Neil I was a Dons fan and I had a confession to make about the evening of 11 May 1983, the night Aberdeen won the European Cup-Winners' Cup. I was watching the game on the big screen in the Nairn County Social Club where the steward, Ian Reside, who did an enormous amount of fund-raising for Nairn, had organised a sweep-stake. I had the ticket for a 1-1 scoreline after 90 minutes. After Eric Black's opener, Real Madrid came back with their spot-kick equaliser. Now, being a true Scot, I got to thinking I could have the best of both worlds here. The prize was £35 – no paltry sum in those days. I confessed to Neil I was hoping for the score to remain 1-1 until 90 minutes and for Aberdeen to bag the winner in extra-time. Selfish I know but – hey – needs must. My wishes were granted when John Hewitt headed the winner in extra-time. I don't know if I went down in Neil's estimation but we had a laugh and went out in the second half and won our friendly match.

And, of course, Davy Johnston was not the only Nairn County player to make his mark at Pittodrie. Two of Neil's team-mates that night in Gothenburg had been rising stars at Station Park, and they were nurtured by Innes Macdonald before their departure to Pittodrie. Eric Black, of course, scored the Dons' opening goal and on the subs' bench was Bryan 'Ben' Gunn. Even as a youngster, Eric's ability to hang in the air that extra second when he leapt for the ball was one of his hallmarks. Bryan, too, was clearly destined for a big future in the game. They were both fine lads and deserved their success.

Another Station Park export to Pittodrie earlier in the 1970s was Ian Gibson, a son of the manse. His father, the Rev A Cameron Gibson, was minister of the Parish Church in Nairn. He was a vet by profession and I believe a Grade I referee before accepting the call to the church. He also wrote books about his life as a vet and in the ministry. He didn't keep in the best of health and moved to a smaller charge at Lockerbie in the

Scottish borders, and was there on that dreadful night of 21 December 1988 when Pan-Am Flight 103 was blown out of the sky. Ian was an amazing player who was almost impossible to dispossess – I can speak from personal experience because I played in the same school team with him at Nairn Academy. His skills were honed with all his mates in a small football pitch at the rear of his dad's church.

Ian Gibson had three brothers, Neil, David and Alan – all talented footballers, too. Neil and David both went on to play for Nairn County and David had spells with Caley and Buckie Thistle. Before his sixteenth birthday Ian starred for Nairn in a pre-season friendly against a Hibs side featuring Pat Stanton and Eric Schaedler. I remember that on one mazy run he left both of these vastly experienced international defenders in his wake as he dribbled through on goal, only to run out of puff and shoot tamely into the keeper's arms. But his talent was spotted and he was signed by Aberdeen, where he became a first-team regular during Jimmy Bonthrone's reign at Pittodrie. Ian, though, was determined to pursue a career in teaching and he later took the opportunity to emigrate and join a former team-mate, Aberdeen defender George Murray, at the Bruce Stadium in Canberra, where he combined both teaching and playing football.

I combined my work involvement with St Ninian with playing Welfare football in the summer. In the early years I played in a pub side with Rod Clyne. I was about eighteen, Rod was in his late 40s, but the adage that youth and experience often gelled did not prove true for the Millford Hotel team. We were too youthful and too experienced and I was our leading goalscorer for the season with three goals. I won't go into the goals-against tally. But I later played in another Welfare team, the Canteen, alongside Neil and David Gibson, where we enjoyed some success, then moved on to the Nairn County Social Club.

Davy Johnston's record as a manager with St Ninian was unrivalled. When he joined us at the start of the 1977-78 season we had been through a traumatic year. He was to win the title in 1977-78 and 1978-79 and, importantly, gave the north section a team that was challenging the east section clubs, including the top Aberdeen sides, at every turn in inter-regional competitions. It was our one disappointment that we failed, however, to win the annual play-off between the champions of the two leagues, and inexplicably collapsed in other inter-regional competitions in the final.

In February 1978 in the Dryborough Cup we defeated Formartine United 3-2. The Aberdeenshire club's very existence in those days was down to the enthusiasm of its elderly president, Eddie Edmond, whose love of the game never diminished in his advancing years. The club, like several other junior teams, has since established itself in the Highland League but, without stalwarts like Eddie, teams such as Formartine would have faded into obscurity. In the next two rounds we were paired with the two clubs regarded as the giants of junior football in Aberdeen.

We saw off the challenge of Sunnybank before a large crowd at Nairn County's ground, Station Park, winning 4-1, only to find Banks o' Dee waiting for us in the semi-finals. Willie Barron scored two outstanding goals in that game and our captain Raymond Sharp, an uncle of Ronnie Sharp who was later to make his mark in the Highland League, was a commanding figure in defence when the Dee turned the screw in the second half. We finished 2-0 winners and, having dispensed with these two big-name sides, we went into the final at Borough Briggs against St Machar with confidence, having already secured the league championship. But a goal in 30 seconds rocked St Ninian and we never recovered from that blow and finished the competition with a whimper, crashing to a 0-4 defeat.

We defeated another Aberdeenshire side, Parkvale, 4-3 in a replay to reach the semi-finals of another inter-regional tournament – the Morrison Trophy – where we were faced with the daunting prospect of a home tie with the east section's Division One champions, East End. Against all the odds we overcame the best side in the Aberdeenshire ranks that season, beating them 3-2 at Nairn on Sunday, 28 May. The following Saturday the tables were reversed when East End beat Saints 2-0 in the annual play-off between the champions of the east section and the champions of the north. Further disappointment was to follow when we lost 1-2 to Ellon United in the final of the Morrison Trophy.

But in Davy's first season in management he had guided St Ninian to a league title, a Stewart Memorial Trophy cup final victory, and two regional cup finals.

More success was to follow in 1978-79 when Davy guided the club to a league title again and a Tom Gordon Trophy win. Success, however, eluded us again in the showdowns with the clubs from the east coast. We lost 2-3 to Formartine in the semi-final of the Morrison Trophy and Banks o' Dee got revenge for their Dryborough Cup defeat the previous year with an 8-2 rout in the inter-regional play-off. Charlie Barbour, who went on to become a prolific scorer in the Highland League, was on fire that day and had Dee 2-0 up within seven minutes. He finished the afternoon with four of his side's eight goals. Our last game of the 1978-79 season was on Saturday, 19 May. With the league championship already in the bag, and holidays and injuries to contend with, we were faced with a

makeshift side for the trip to play Rothes Decimals in the heart of
Speyside whisky country. I had to make up the numbers by taking a seat
on the bench. Fourteen year-old Ian Thain, who went on to have a long
and distinguished career in the Highland League with Keith, appeared as
a substitute goalkeeper, replacing Ian Findlay for the last 25 minutes.

Davy Johnston pulled on his boots for what was to be one of his rare
appearances for Saints. Fittingly he was on the scoresheet in the match,
which was drawn 2-2. Davy's goal was a cool chip over the advancing
Rothes keeper. Despite my enthusiasm to get on the park, even for five
minutes, just to say I was a member of the league-winning side that season, I wasn't brought on. I even tried to bribe Davy by promising him to
buy him a pint after the game, but he was having none of it.

Dougie Storm, whose brother George played with Nairn County during Davy's spell at Station Park, was a prolific scorer with Saints during
the 1977-78 and 1978-79 title-winning seasons during Davy's tenure
before joining Forres Mechanics. He is convinced that Davy could have
gone on to make his mark as a manager in the Highland League because
he still had so much to offer:

'I grew up with a ball at my feet and Davy was my sporting hero,'
Dougie recalls. 'I wrote him a letter when he was at Aberdeen asking for
his and the rest of the team's autographs and he replied with a hand written letter and all the autographs I had asked for. I treasured that letter for
many years. Like most of the lads in the St Ninian team, we had followed
his career from a distance but never in my wildest dreams did I think he
would become a manager of a team I was to play for. It was his unpre-
tentious manner which put the players at ease and we responded to him.
He was a great motivator and spoke to us collectively and individually and
made you feel ten feet tall before you went out on to that pitch. It's little
wonder we were so successful and we were all convinced it was only
going to be a matter of time before he was snapped up to manage a
Highland League club, but he really wasn't interested in moving on. He
loved the banter of the training pitch and on rain-soaked evenings at the
Showfield his class shone through. We would struggle to keep our feet
but Davy, wearing only sandshoes, displayed a poise and balance which
was the hallmark of a great player. And, despite all his achievements in
the game, never once did I hear him talk about himself, about scoring this
goal or that goal or playing before more than 126,000-odd fans against
Celtic at Hampden.'

It was in November 1979 that Davy Johnston resigned from St Ninian
'for personal reasons'. He had been reunited with his wife Margaret. They
remarried in April of that year and their youngest son Trevor was born.

His daughter Sharon and eldest son David had been travelling with their dad to all of our games and it came as no surprise to the committee when he quit the club to resume family life. We were resigned to the fact we were losing a superb manager. But we were also grateful for having had him for these two seasons, which yielded so much success.

Gordon Ingram took over the managerial reins for a short spell and just missed out on the title. He was succeeded by Billy Douglas, another star of the Highland League, who guided the club to the championship in 1981-82. Dave Cochrane followed in the managerial chair and while cup success continued, the title has continued to elude St Ninian.

Davy Johnston returned to the Showfield in the mid-1980s with another club stalwart, Jeff Mackintosh, as his assistant. They were to bring together a new crop of players, including Ronnie Sharp. Ronnie was a fantastic hurdler in his young days and at an international meet in Colwyn Bay when he was a schoolboy he beat a certain young Welsh hurdler. His name was Colin Jackson, who went on to win the 110-metres Olympic silver medal and become world champion. But football was Ronnie's first love. He later played for Nairn County and was manager at Station Park, where he brought the club back to a respectable position in the league before he was replaced by present manager Les Fridge, the former Chelsea and St Mirren goalkeeper. Ronnie was a gifted footballer and is now manager at the Showfield, and although in his mid-40s still plays, using his experience playing at sweeper.

Davy Johnston's second spell with the club in 1984-85 was not as successful as his first, but he left in the knowledge he had introduced some new young blood for future managers.

Between his two managerial spells, Davy played some Welfare League football for Ardersier, but when he retired from St Ninian for the last time he disappeared into obscurity and became almost reclusive, rarely venturing out from his home in Auldearn, apart from work and visits to his ageing mother in Nairn. Even when his son Trevor began to show great promise on the football field with the village side, Davy never ventured out to see him play. One of his greatest pleasures was smoking his pipe, which he only did privately in his own home. His only contact with the sport he loved was through the television and newspapers, in particular the *Green Final*, which he read avidly and kept faithfully in touch with events at Pittodrie.

It was also with great sadness, not long after my return with my family from a spell in Australia, that I learned that Davy's son David had been diagnosed with cancer. A quiet lad, he was a popular local taxi driver. He passed away at the age of 30 in 1997.

Tributes (and Memories) from Pittodrie Legends

HARRY MELROSE was on the bench as team coach when Davy Johnston and Ian Taylor wrecked Rangers' title dream in 1968. Turnbull was a great admirer of Melrose and he was one of his first signings as he looked for the building blocks of his new side. By the end of the 1968-69 season Harry's playing days were over. Turnbull, though, saw him as a valued lieutenant with a great deal still to contribute and he appointed him as a coach at Pittodrie to replace Davie Shaw after he retired.

Harry recalls the mayhem after Ian Taylor's winning goal in that unforgettable match against Rangers: 'Eddie had been priming the boys up all week. They all knew how much it meant to the club getting into Europe and every Aberdeen player in that game was outstanding. I think it was Martin [Buchan] who passed the ball to Davy in the middle of the park in the final minute of the game and he battered up that wing with that incredible pace of his before turning the ball back into Ian's path and he just let fly, giving their keeper no chance. Eddie, Tommy [Craig] and myself had to fight each other to get out of the small dugout to celebrate and we tripped over each other in the excitement trackside. It was a wonderful feeling.'

As for his thoughts on Davy Johnston, Melrose, who went on to manage Berwick, then Dunfermline for five years before he retired from the game in 1980, had this to say:

'Davy hinted to me he often wanted home. He was a shy lad who would listen but not often contribute when he was out with the players and their wives socially. I think in truth he was a bit overwhelmed by the big city and some of the players he was mixing with. But he was as good as anyone in the League in that era and of course had a tremendous physique which gave him that incredible pace and his awesome shooting power. Eddie played him principally on the right wing but he could also play through the middle.

'But when you look back on it, 37 goals in 99 games is an excellent return for a winger. The football pitch was where Davy could best express himself. It was a situation where he felt he was on a par with everyone else and I think deep down there was always an underlying lack of self-confidence. The great outside-right that so many Aberdeen fans remember is Graham Leggat. He must have been some player if he was better than Davy Johnston.'

Martin Buchan's family name is synonymous with Aberdeen Football Club. Martin Buchan was just seventeen on Davy's arrival at Pittodrie in 1966. Martin had six years with the Dons and eleven with Manchester United after his transfer for an Aberdeen club record fee of £125,000 in 1972. He was the only player to captain Scottish FA and English FA Cup winning sides. His triumph with the Dons came in 1970 when they dumped Celtic 3-1 in what became known as Cup-tie Mackay's final, because of the scoring exploits of Derek Mackay in the run up to the Hampden showdown, and in the final itself when he bagged two goals. Martin also captained United to a 2-1 victory over Liverpool in the 1977 FA Cup final and was capped by Scotland 34 times during his career, playing in the 1974 and 1978 World Cup finals. His father, also Martin, brother George and son Jamie, all had spells with the Dons.

Martin Buchan shared Davy's high and lows throughout his Pittodrie career, but their time together was not without its lighter moments. Anyone who knew Davy would be aware that he had no interest in cars and never held a driving licence in his life – unlike the high rollers in the sport today. But Martin recalls one of the funniest stories of the times they shared together in the Granite City when Davy nearly got lifted for dangerous driving:

'Davy was getting a lift to training in Jens Petersen's car. Jens, of course, was from Denmark and he lived next door to Davy in Cairnfield Place. Davy was sitting in the passenger seat with his arms folded, looking over and chatting away to Jens when they turned a corner and were stopped by a policeman who almost threw himself on the bonnet to bring the car to a screeching halt. The bobby produced his notebook and was about to charge Davy with dangerous driving because he didn't have his hands on the steering wheel as they turned the corner. It was only then that the penny dropped – Jens' car was a left-hand drive. Exit one very embarrassed policeman.'

It was a story Davy loved to tell over a pint with his team-mates. 'We loved his accent,' said Martin. 'He was really good company and was well-liked by all his team-mates.' Martin's own views on Davy's departure from the Dons really coincides with what I have heard over and over again in my research for this book:

'I think the reason Davy left the Dons was because he never really felt settled in Aberdeen. I always got the impression that he missed the simpler life he'd had up north. Less pressure maybe, because even in those days there were high expectations to meet if you were a professional footballer. And I don't think he ever realised how good a player he was. I had the privilege of playing with Bobby Charlton and I once said that

Bobby was the only genuine two-footed player I've seen, but I've got to say that Davy ran him close. He had big, powerful thighs and he could fairly strike a ball, but he was a clever, skilful player as well.'

Martin also recalls the unforgettable tour of Canada and the US in 1967 and the horrible injury Davy sustained in that match against Uruguayan side Cerro: 'He took a full set of studs from a thug and it ripped his leg open, exposing the calf muscle. Fortunately we had an excellent American doctor called George Resta who took good care of him, but I'll never forget the state of his leg when we went to help him when he went down. Davy was popular with all the lads and we were all very sorry when he left Pittodrie. I am sure he could have gone on to greater things.'

Buchan now works for the Professional Footballers Association based in Manchester, where he made his home after his playing days ended.

IAN TAYLOR should have had cause for consternation at Davy Johnston's arrival at Pittodrie. For it was he who Davy often displaced leading the forward line. But Ian's admiration for Johnston was undiminished: 'I preferred playing through the middle but often the boss preferred Davy playing there alongside Jim Storrie, although he played often on both wings as well. It was understandable. Davy was older and had lots of experience at Highland League level and had already played in the First Division with Hearts.

'Martin [Buchan] and I joined together from Banks o' Dee. We were both only lads of seventeen, while Davy was already married with a young family, so we didn't mix socially a great deal. But he was a great team-mate.'

Now semi-retired, working as a consultant in the offshore oil supply industry, Ian was with the Dons for eight years before moving to Motherwell, where he played alongside Peter Marinello and Willie Pettigrew, finishing his career at Perth with St Johnstone. He recalls the fateful Scottish Cup final of 1967 when Aberdeen lost 0-2 to soon-to-be crowned European Champions Celtic:

'Anything that could go wrong that day did go wrong. Eddie Turnbull was very ill and was confined to his bed in our hotel in Gleneagles. I recall the boys were even taken to his room so he could name the team, then we were left in the hands of our trainer Davie Shaw who was in charge at Hampden and Harry Melrose was captain. I was named as a substitute and Davy was playing at outside-left. In those days there was only one substitute and they were not allowed to be used for tactical reasons. You would only get on if someone was injured so I never played.

'The team bus even arrived late at Hampden Park. We didn't get there until 45 minutes before kick-off. Here we were, preparing for the biggest game of our lives, with no manager and, of course, the tension was building up on the team bus as we fought our way through the traffic to get to the ground. We should have been there by 1.30. No one had thought there would be such a massive support down from Aberdeen that day and the route to Hampden was choc-a-bloc with buses and cars from the north. It was very much the people's game in those days but it's gone corporate now.

'We just never performed that day. It was a non-event for us and we had worked so hard to get there. Losing 0-2 was a disappointment but three weeks later Celtic were crowned European Champions, so all things considered we were not disgraced. You have to remember this was a golden era for Scottish football. There were many fine teams around and the international side oozed class. But it didn't ease the pain of losing in a Cup final. We had already started our tour in America when we heard Celtic had beaten Inter-Milan and we were delighted for them.'

Ian, like Martin Buchan, recalled the tackle which everyone thought had ended Davy's tour. 'It was crude, one of the dirtiest challenges I've ever seen on a football pitch. You could see the muscle hanging through his stocking and he was carted off to hospital. We all visited Davy to cheer him up and he told us his tour was finished. But when the boss came in, Davy was playing a different tune and said he would be back soon. And he was. The doctor who treated the injury did an amazing job and he was back playing within two to three weeks.

'Relations between Eddie [Turnbull] and all the players were often strained. It wasn't just with Davy. He liked it that way, I suppose, to keep us on our toes.'

One of the best moments they shared was that 3-2 victory over Rangers on the last day of the 1967-68 season: 'I still visit Eddie occasionally and the topic of Davy Johnston often crops up. He believes he could have been a world beater. Davy wasn't tall but he was very stocky and he could punch his weight in any company. He had two great feet and was powerful in the air.

'The only criticism I have of Davy is he didn't realise how good he was and there was a consensus that he would have gone on to play for Scotland. It shouldn't be forgotten either that this was in an era when you had the likes of Dennis Law, Jimmy Johnstone, Jim Baxter, Willie Henderson and Willie Johnston all on the international scene. To give it all up and go back to Nairn, he must have felt deep down that for him there were better things in life than football.'

As a postscript, Ian recalled a story to me after Davy's departure from Aberdeen which was a reflection of the high regard Turnbull had for the Highland League. In 1971 his Dons side were drawn at home to Elgin City in the Scottish Cup. The Dons were the Cup holders and Turnbull was determined nothing should be left to chance:

'We blew the League on the run in that season,' recalled Ian, 'but when we got City in the Cup Eddie knew we would have to be at our best. Ally Shewan was playing for Elgin by then and we knew he would certainly do us no favours. As luck would have it, on the Saturday we were due to play, there was a slight frost and Eddie was on edge. We had all gone for our pre-match meal when the boss came in and told us there was some doubt about the game going ahead. The reality was Eddie didn't want to take any chances and the ref was called in. We went down to Pittodrie and Eddie came off the pitch smiling and with his thumbs up when the ref called the game off. I don't know to this day if Eddie had said anything to the ref. If he did, he's never going to own up to it but I know he was desperate not to play. I had certainly played on a lot worse and we even trained on the pitch that afternoon. We beat Elgin 5-1 the following Monday on a perfect pitch before a crowd of 25,000. At that time the Highland League was very strong, with Caley another team to be reckoned with.

ALLY SHEWAN is probably the player best placed to tell us more about the enigmatic Johnston. He was his closest pal during his spell at Pittodrie. Now retired and living in Peterhead, Ally enjoyed a second career in the oil industry after his time with the Dons during the late 1960s, when he was an ever-present in the side. They roomed together whenever their games involved overnight stays and a strong friendship was forged on that memorable tour of the States during Davy's first summer with the Dons. They were to renew that camaraderie years later when their playing careers at the top level were over and they worked together at the McDermott's oil yard at Ardersier:

'To some extent we were kindred spirits,' said Ally. 'Like me, Davy came from the country. I was walking out of the stadium after training the day Davy arrived to be shown round for the first time after he signed from Nairn County. I knew he was a country lad like myself and I knew he would be nervous about joining a big club like Aberdeen. So I made a point of going up to him and shaking his hand and welcoming him to Aberdeen. I befriended him and as team captain I made a point of helping him settle in and talked through with him what it entailed to become a full-time footballer.

'He came across as a shy lad needing a bit of guidance. But from the first time I saw him training I realised his potential and what a rare talent he was. I was determined we were not going to let it slide and did everything I could to make him feel at home. When I heard a book was being written as a tribute to him I was delighted. He was a legend and my best friend. I was just surprised that no one had put Davy's story into print before. As a footballer and an athlete he was one of the lucky guys to be born with a natural talent. Players like me had to work damned hard to get where we were in the game, but for Davy it came naturally.'

Shewan was regarded as one of the most loyal and dependable defenders in the Scottish game during the 1960s. He made 300 appearances for the Dons and scored nine goals and left the club in 1969, the same year as Davy, over a contractual dispute. Ally confirmed that Davy found the transition to full-time training took its toll:

'He was often physically sick because he could not handle the training Eddie put us through. He hated training but the truth was he didn't need the same training as the rest of us because he was a natural athlete. I was a different kettle of fish. I loved training. I was the type of player who needed to be pushed. I was captain for a few years and I was determined that I would lead by example. The only player on a par with me or perhaps even fitter was our goalkeeper, Bobby Clark. Eddie would tell me to take the boys round on circuits and Davy would just shake his head – "not him again" – I could hear him say under his breath. To tell the truth, I was envious because he was such a natural. He could have walked into any team but he just needed that confidence and that's all he lacked.'

Ally said Davy was the only player in the squad, with the exception of Harry Melrose, who called him by his nickname 'Neebs'. 'Harry came to us from Dunfermline and it was him who started calling me Neebs. I don't know if it was a Fife expression. For all I know it might have been less than complimentary and I've never taken the trouble to find out what it meant. But Davy was the only member of the squad who used my nickname.' Neebs, in fact, is a Fife expression meaning 'neighbour'.

Ally recalled that the last time he met up with his old team boss was when they were honoured by Aberdeen Football Club and inducted to the club's hall of fame: 'We had a lovely dinner and stayed overnight with our wives at a local hotel. In the morning we had breakfast together with our wives who had to put up with us as the conversation inevitably turned to football. Davy's name came up and Eddie told me that the best kicker of a ball he ever saw as a player or manager was Davy Johnston. What a compliment that was, coming from one of Scotland's greatest ever coaches and a player who was a member of the most famous forward lines

Scotland has ever known. Davy virtually needed no backlift to deliver a shot with incredible power. And he also had an unbelievable burst of speed and his other very rare attribute – he was as strong with his left foot as he was with his right.

'Eddie was one of the best judges of a player and I know he said Davy could have been as good as Bobby Charlton. Personally I would say he would have been better than Bobby Charlton if he had become a senior footballer and received the proper coaching at an earlier age. It's a pity he never stuck it with Hearts. But on reflection I would never have had the good fortune to play alongside him and have him as a friend, and on both counts that was a great privilege.'

Ally, too, recalled the trip to the USA which for the entire Aberdeen squad was a once in a lifetime experience. Sharing a room with Davy, it was an opportunity to get to know him better: 'My admiration for him as a player was growing by the day. He was growing in confidence with every game until that sickening tackle in the game against the Uruguayan team. The final, though, with Wolves was an unforgettable match. There was no holding back from either side and there were some right personal battles going on all over the pitch. I had orders at the start from Eddie to put Derek Dougan in his place. He was an amazing player, vastly under-rated in my view but certainly not by Eddie. Early in the game I managed to give him a good dig in the kidneys when he came up for a corner. Ten minutes later he put me out cold with a head butt when the ref wasn't looking. I came round a few minutes later and Derek was there with an outstretched hand helping me up. "I know you were put up to it, now let's play football," he said. There was another big stramash involving "Chalky" White, Jimmy Smith and Dave Wagstaffe and at one time Jimmy ran off the pitch on to the terracing with Wagstaffe in hot pursuit. There was no hatred after the final whistle and we had a good laugh when someone remarked: "No wonder this place is called the Colosseum".'

Not long after Davy dropped his bombshell that he was quitting Aberdeen in 1969, Ally too decided it was time to seek pastures new: 'When I started my career in 1959-60, I was earning £14 a week and a win bonus would take me up to £18. Tradesmen were earning £10 a week, so we couldn't complain.'

Although he admits it was disillusionment over the terms he was being offered by Aberdeen which prompted him to move on from the club he had lived and breathed for a whole decade, Shewan is in no doubt that the game has been spoiled by the cash rewards that are available today: 'It's not envy. I had a wonderful career in football and I've had a wonderful life since and met many great people and I'm happy with my lot. Players no longer play for the jersey. We had to be in the team to earn the money. Now they just get a contract and see their bank balance grow.'

When the parting of the ways came with the Dons, it was off to Australia to seek fame and fortune. He found neither and happily returned to the north of Scotland, where he found employment at McDermott's and his footballing services in big demand in the Highland League. He played for Elgin City, where he spent three seasons before joining Ross County for a short spell. After finishing at Victoria Park he got a team of welders and fitter fabricators together from McDermott's and they became the Nairn Welfare League champions to add to the championship medal he won with Elgin in 1969-70. He returned to Elgin in a coaching capacity. His time in the Highland League put him in the unique position that he got to know Davy as an adversary as well as a team-mate:

'Playing against him was murder because of his speed, his balance and instant ball control. There was one cup semi-final we played against Caley at Kingsmills and Davy was trying to get away from me. I thought "you bugger, you're not getting away from me this time" and I went in high and took him down. I was hard but never dirty. I knew my tackle would stop him but not injure him. He was a totally honest player who would take a knock and dust himself down, unlike the modern footballers of today who will take a dive to gain any advantage. He was as complete a footballer any manager could wish to have. The only thing Davy lacked was self-belief and self-confidence and nothing we could do or say would convince him otherwise. But Eddie always said signing Davy from Nairn was one of the best pieces of business he ever did as a manager.'

Epilogue

Most of us can reflect on our lives on missed opportunities, wrong choices and decisions we've made which we may look back on with regret if things haven't panned out the way we would have hoped. But at the end of the day, many of the choices we have made were the right ones. We have taken personal responsibility for them after much forethought.

I know that's true of me, the same as it is of anyone else, and these decisions and life choices have contributed to the person I am today. Had I opted to give up journalism and pursue a career in the oil sector when it presented itself in the early 1970s, I certainly wouldn't be in the privileged position I find myself sitting here, recording the career of one of Highland football's all-time greats. Davy, I sincerely believe, never had any regrets about the choices he made in football. If he did, he never expressed them to me or anyone else I have spoken to.

He knew his own comfort zone and chose to remain within it, and in doing so he followed a path where he was able to continue to play and enjoy the sport he loved. He tasted life at the top level of Scottish football, saw a bit of the world, and played before a packed Hampden stadium in front of 126,000 fans. He proved to himself and his army of fans in the Highlands he could hold his own against the best Scottish football had to offer in a golden era for the game in this small country of ours. The sport he enjoyed never brought him financial riches. But I believe it brought him far more than that. For the fans who remember him, too, he has left behind many wonderful memories.

In writing this book, I was acutely aware that Davy Johnston's story had never been fully told nor recorded. Unfortunately, young people never tend to see their parents, if they are sporting heroes, at the height of their powers. Through the good offices of Aberdeen Football Club Heritage Trust I have been able to obtain some footage of the 1967 Scottish Cup final and the President's Cup. I hope that footage and this book will provide Davy's surviving children, Sharon, Kevin, Jacqueline and Trevor, with something tangible for their dad's contribution to the beautiful game here in the Highlands.

'Be not afraid of greatness: some are born great, some achieve greatness and some have greatness thrust upon them'. Act 11, Scene V, Shakespeare's Play *Twelfth Night*.

Davy Johnston timeline

28 November 1942. Davy Johnston born.

28 February 1959. Nairn County debut in North of Scotland Cup second round. Nairn lost 0-2 at Station Park.

15 April 1959. Scores first of 279 goals (approx) for Nairn in 2-0 win against Clach at Grant Street.

29 October 1960. Joins Hearts.

12 November 1960. Scottish League debut for Hearts at Kilmarnock. Hearts win 2-1.

1 April 1961. First Scottish League goal in 1-1 draw with Raith Rovers at Starks Park. Later walks out on Hearts.

14 October 1961. Hearts release Davy from his contract with them 'for personal reasons' and he appears for Nairn County at Lossie. No fairytale return, as Nairn lose 1-2.

1963-64. New Nairn club record of 73 goals, which for over four decades people thought was a Highland League record for one season.

7 November 1966. Joins Aberdeen, three weeks before 24th birthday.

17 December 1966. Recently turned 24, makes his Aberdeen first-team debut after scoring in every game for reserves. Scores a goal and lays on two more in a 6-2 win against Stirling Albion at Annfield.

24 December 1966. Old Firm debut against Celtic. 1-1 draw at Pittodrie before 28,000 fans.

1 February 1967. Scores first hat-trick for Dons in 7-0 home win over Airdrie.

29 April 1967. Scottish Cup final appearance against Celtic before 126,000 fans at Hampden Park. Celtic won 2-0.

14 July 1967. President's Cup final against Wolves in Los Angeles. Wolves win thriller 6-5 with a deciding golden goal after extra-time.

27 April 1968. Davy scores two goals and lays on the winner in the final minute in 3-2 over Rangers at Ibrox. This result killed off Rangers' title hopes and secured Aberdeen a place in Europe.

23 April 1969. Davy's last competitive game for Aberdeen – a 1-1 draw with Clyde at Shawfield. The Dons had just fought off relegation. Davy later walks out on the club.

2 August 1969. Davy returns to the Highland League and makes his debut for Caley in a 1-0 friendly win at Montrose.

1970-71. Wins first Highland League medal with Caley.

17 May 1972. Davy scores two goals in friendly against Ranger FC in testimonial game. Rangers won the friendly 5-2, and the following week they won the European Cup-Winners' Cup.

27 July 1972. Chic Allan's death stuns north football.

April 1975. Davy walks out on Caley.

October 1975. Davy returns to Nairn. Expected to play on 4 October in a cup-tie against Keith, but SFA mislaid his registration papers. Played on 11 October in 1-2 defeat at Lossiemouth. Went on to play twelve games in Nairn's first ever league-winning season.

28 February 1976. Scores his last goal for Nairn in 3-1 win against Peterhead.

6 March 1976. Plays last game for Nairn against Keith and retires from senior football.

August 1977. Becomes manager of Nairn St Ninian FC. Guides them to two successive league championships before resigning in November 1979.

1984-85. In charge again for a year at St Ninian. Season ends with two cup final defeats and no trophies.

7 April 2004. Davy, 61, passed away in Highland Hospice, Inverness.

PLAYING HONOURS:

Nairn County: North of Scotland Cup, 1963-64, 1965-66; Highland League Cup 1963-64, Highland League 1975-76.

Aberdeen: Scottish Cup runners-up 1967; USA President's Cup runners-up 1967.

Inverness Caledonian: North of Scotland Cup 1973-74; Highland League Cup 1969-70, 1971-72; Scottish Qualifying Cup (North) 1969-70, 1971-72; Highland League 1970-71.

MANAGERIAL HONOURS:

Nairn St Ninian North Regional League (North) Section Champions 1977-78, 1978-79. Stewart Memorial Trophy 1977-78. Tom Gordon Trophy 1978-79.

CLUB PLAYING AND SCORING RECORDS (excluding friendlies):

NAIRN COUNTY:

1958-59 Played 10, goals 3.
1959-60 Played 38, goals 12.
1960-61 Played 12, goals 9 (before joining Hearts).
1961-62 Played 17, goals 17 (on his return from Hearts).
1962-63 Played 47, goals 47.
1963-64 Played 46, goals 73.
1964-65 Played 37, goals 43.
1965-66 Played 44, goals 61.
1966-67 Played 15, goals 19 (before joining Aberdeen).
1975-76 Played 13, goals 2.

Total games played for Nairn County 279, goals scored 286.

INVERNESS CALEY:

1969-70 Played 42, goals 51.
1970-71 Played 36, goals 39.
1971-72 Played 39, goals 33.
1972-73 Played 18, goals 11.
1973-74 Played 24, goals 12.
1974-75 Played 29, goals 10.

Total games played for Caley 188, goals scored 156.
Statistics provided by Caley historian Ian Davidson.

ABERDEEN:

1966-67 Played 26, goals 14.
1967-68 Played 36, goals 14.
1968-69 Played 37, goals 9.

Total games played for Aberdeen 99, goals 37.

HEARTS:

1961-62 Played 5, goals 1.

Career totals: Played 571 games, 480 goals (excluding friendlies).

QUICKEST GOALS:

20 seconds in a 6-3 win for Nairn County against Wick Academy at Station Park on 24 September 1960 in a Qualifying Cup replay. Davy scored five goals that day and the following month joined Hearts.

40 seconds in a 2-0 win for Aberdeen against Dundee at Dens Park on 1 January 1968.